PRESIDENTIAL POWER
AND
MANAGEMENT TECHNIQUES

**Recent Titles in
Contributions in Political Science
Series Editor: Bernard K. Johnpoll**

PRESIDENTIAL POWER

AND

MANAGEMENT TECHNIQUES

*The Carter and Reagan Administrations
in Historical Perspective*

JAMES G. BENZE, JR.

JK
518
.B47
1987
WEST

Contributions in Political Science,
Number 175

GREENWOOD PRESS
New York • Westport, Connecticut • London

Library of Congress Cataloging-in-Publication Data

Benze, James G.
  Presidential power and management techniques.

  (Contributions in political science, ISSN 0147-1066 ;
no. 175)
    Bibliography: p.
    Includes index.
    1. Presidents—United States—Staff. 2. United
States—Executive departments—Management. 3. United
States—Politics and government—1977–1981. 4. United
States—Politics and government—1981–   . I. Title.
II. Series.
JK518.B47 1987   353.03'23   87-233
ISBN 0-313-25601-2 (lib. bdg. : alk. paper)

British Library Cataloguing in Publication Data is available.

Library of Congress Catalog Card Number: 87-233
ISBN: 0-313-25601-2
ISSN: 0147-1066

First published in 1987

Greenwood Press, Inc.
88 Post Road West, Westport, Connecticut 06881

Printed in the United States of America

The paper used in this book complies with the
Permanent Paper Standard issued by the National
Information Standards Organization (Z39.48-1984).

10 9 8 7 6 5 4 3 2 1

To my wife Pamela
and my Mother and Father

Contents

Tables

Abbreviations

AAA	Agricultural Adjustment Administration
BOB	Bureau of the Budget
CCA	Cabinet Council on Administration
CCEA	Cabinet Council on Economic Affairs
CCHR	Cabinet Council on Human Resources
CCLAM	Cabinet Council on Legal Affairs and Management
CCNRE	Cabinet Council on Natural Resources and Environment
CCFA	Cabinet Council on Food and Agriculture
CCCT	Cabinet Council on Commerce and Trade
EOP	Executive Office of the President
ERDA	Energy Research and Development Administration
FEA	Federal Energy Administration
HEW	Health, Education, and Welfare
HUD	Housing and Urban Development
MBO	Management by Objectives
NRA	National Recovery Administration
OIRA	Office of Information and Regulatory Affairs
OMB	Office of Management and Budget
POSDCORB	Planning, Organizing, Staffing, Directing, Coordinating, Reporting, Budgeting

PCAM	President's Commission on Administrative Management
PPBS	Planned Program Budgeting System
RIA	Regulatory Impact Analysis
RIF	Reduction in Force
SES	Senior Executive Service
WPA	Works Progress Administration
ZBB	Zero Base Budgeting

Acknowledgments

In writing this book, I have become indebted to a large number of people. David A. Caputo, Robert Sahr, and Dean Knudsen read early drafts of the manuscript, and the final copy is much better for their advice.

My greatest intellectual debt is owed to Myron Q. Hale, who has greatly influenced my thoughts on presidential power and presidential management. The material on presidential power in Chapter 1 has been shamelessly borrowed from his own work. I am grateful that he was so generous with his ideas.

I am also, of course, grateful to the numerous civil servants who participated in not just one, but two mail surveys. Without their help and valuable insight, this book would not have been possible.

I would also like to thank two people whose impact, while less direct, was nonetheless important. Rodney Hero and Eugene Declercq were the friends who helped me through the rough moments.

Finally, no list of acknowledgments would be complete without mentioning my wife Pamela. Not only was she kind, patient, and understanding during very trying times, but quite literally without her editorial skills, this book might not have been completed. In terms of level of commitment, the book is as much hers as mine.

Of course, while all of the above contributed mightily, I take sole responsibility for the ideas presented in this book.

PRESIDENTIAL POWER
AND
MANAGEMENT TECHNIQUES

Introduction

Modern presidents have expressed dissatisfaction with their inability to control policy implementation by the federal bureaucracy. President Franklin D. Roosevelt complained:

The Treasury is so large and far-flung and ingrained in its practices that I find it is almost impossible to get the action and results that I want. . . . But the Treasury is not to be compared with the State Department. You should go through the experience of trying to get any changes in the thinking, policy and action of the career diplomats and then you'd know what a real problem was. But the Treasury and the State Department put together are nothing compared with the Na-a-vy.[1]

President John F. Kennedy once compared the State Department to a bowl of jelly, and he complained, "It's got all those people over there who are constantly smiling. I think we need to smile less and be tougher."[2] President Richard M. Nixon referred to his opponents in the bureaucracy as "dug-in establishmentarians fighting for the status quo," and he thought it "repugnant to the American system that only the bureaucratic elite at the top of the heap in Washington believes it knows what is best for the people."[3]

With varying degrees of success, each modern president has employed different strategies to gain greater control over the bureaucracy and the implementation of his policies. Franklin Roosevelt relied heavily on reorganization, staffing, and administrative management; President Harry S Truman made extensive use of his cabinet officers in both advisory and management capacities; President Dwight D. Eisenhower developed a highly formalized staff system relying heavily on his chief of staff; John Kennedy used his senior White House staff to oversee the bureaucracy; President Lyndon B. Johnson relied on his political executives and innovations in budgeting, in addition to his own brand of leadership; and Richard Nixon manipulated political appointees and the career civil service and introduced new management programs to agency budgeting.

Taken together, these management strategies represent a historical trend toward centralization of policy implementation in the office of the chief executive. This historical trend is presidential management, and it consists of a variety of administrative techniques, some of which date from Franklin Roosevelt's terms and some of which are relatively new. This research studies the development of this trend toward increased presidential control over the bureaucracy and evaluates the successes and failures of presidential management from Franklin Roosevelt to Presidents Jimmy Carter and Ronald Reagan. This research also considers the reasons for effective presidential management.

Earlier studies of management in the executive branch focused on a single administrative technique, such as budgeting or reorganization, used in only one administration. This research investigates a variety of administrative techniques under the general concept of presidential management. Studying the totality of presidential management reveals the relations among various administrative techniques, as well as the development of the trend toward centralization of administrative power in the executive. It also highlights the similarity among the principles and purposes underlying these administrative techniques.

This research is primarily concerned with the relationship between presidential power and presidential management. Relating power and management suggests the political importance of administrative techniques in a normative fashion. This is particularly significant in light of recent discussion and examination of the administrative and management aspects of presidential power.

This research also provides an empirical investigation of presidential management in the Carter and Reagan administrations. Focusing on the Carter and Reagan management programs adds an immediacy to the research that is not often found in the literature on the presidency. Moreover, the empirical investigation attempts to overcome the many criticisms of the nonempirical presidential literature.

Chapter 1 develops the links between power and management and argues that policy implementation is central to a discussion of presidential power—a notion advanced by identifying sources of presidential power and by distinguishing power from influence and authority.

Chapters 2 and 3 focus on the historical development of presidential management. Chapter 2 argues that presidential management stems not only from the frustrations that presidents experience in confronting a monolithic bureaucracy but also from societal changes such as World Wars I and II and the Great Depression. Development of public administration theory provided the management techniques as well as the rationale for the centralization of administrative power in the chief executive.

Chapter 3 considers the administrative techniques of presidential management, paying particular attention to the problems surrounding their development and the different ways in which they have been applied.

Chapter 4 reviews the major features of the Carter administration and its management programs in the areas of personnel, reorganization, and budgeting. This chapter also addresses the development of presidential management style—the orientation that a president develops toward management—which provides a basis for a comparative study of presidential management.

Chapter 5 reviews the management programs of the Reagan administration, demonstrating a significant shift in the nature of presidential management.

Chapter 6 analyzes the results of an empirical investigation of management in the Carter and Reagan administrations. In 1980 and 1984, questionnaires were sent to administrative and management executives in the major departments and independent agencies in the federal bureaucracy. Their responses are used to evaluate the Carter and Reagan management programs from the perspective of those most affected—the career executives.

Chapter 7 uses statistical analysis to identify the factors most important for the success of a president's management program.

Overall, this research points to the importance of management on the national level. All modern presidents have considered management a necessity, and controlling the federal bureaucracy has been of the utmost importance for Carter and Reagan. Given its historical importance and its current emphasis, a thorough study of presidential management is needed.

NOTES

1. Quoted in Richard M. Pious, *The American Presidency* (New York: Basic Books, 1979), p. 211.

2. Arthur M. Schlesinger, Jr., *A Thousand Days* (New York: Fawcett, 1965), p. 406.

3. Quoted in David A. Caputo and Richard L. Cole, "Presidential Control of the Senior Civil Service: Assessing the Strategies of the Nixon Years," *American Political Science Review*, vol. 73 (June 1979), p. 400.

1

Presidential Power and Presidential Management

Presidential power is closely bound to presidential management. On one hand, the study of presidential power brings a theoretical framework for understanding the origins and limitations of management techniques employed by presidents. On the other hand, the study of presidential management both broadens and deepens the conventional conceptions of presidential power.

There are many reasons for the emergence of presidential management. Throughout the past half-century, the federal bureaucracy has grown in size and importance. The bureaucracy's increased prominence has been expressed in terms of both policy design and policy implementation. As Hugh Heclo suggests, the civil servant has become "an unexpected and insecurely placed participant to the original grand design of American government."[1] As a result, one of the continuing ironies of American politics is that while the bureaucracy provided much of the knowledge and expertise that led to the growth of the modern presidency, it also set boundaries on the choices available to presidents in implementing decisions. As R. G. H. Sin states,

The seasoned bureaucrat is adept at socio-bureaucratic viscosity: to every challenge there is an equal and frustrating viscosity. He dwells in the nirvana of historical momentum: reversing a bureaucrat is tantamount to reversing history. The elected official may represent the prevailing sentiments of the citizens at the time, under the illusion of the election campaign, but the bureaucrats embody the cumulative experience and mores of all the previous elected officials, civil servants and citizen preferences of the past pre-election realities which impart the vector and momentum in the evolution of government. They have the information in their files and the knowledge in their persons which constitutes the essential stuff of power. It is this historical momentum that is the source of the irresistible power in the senior civil servants and ranking military officers. Bureaucrats must be taken as a durable political elite in their own right. Bureaucrats have no fear of democracy.[2]

There are a variety of factors that increase the amount of difficulty presidents experience in attempting to manage the bureaucracy. Of primary importance are the relationships called iron triangles, triple alliances, and subgovernments. These well-developed links between career civil servants, interest group elites, policy elites, and congressional committee elites establish a political power base that allows the agency to resist presidential control.

Another important factor is the ability of particular constituencies to capture agencies and to substitute their interests for the broader presidential interests. The longer tenure of career civil servants creates a longer historical perspective, in which a president's interests become of secondary importance, and increases the difficulty in managing domestic policies.[3] Political scientists have also demonstrated that the bureaucracy may develop an ideology that is hostile to a president's interests and that can be changed only by concerted presidential effort.[4] In addition, the size, complexity, wide-ranging responsibility, and continuity of the federal bureaucracy serve to thwart a president's desires. The control of information and the expertise at the disposal of agency personnel provide an excellent bargaining chip in the continual process of give-and-take with the president's representatives.

Modern presidents have sought to increase their control over the bureaucracy through management techniques. Among these techniques are reorganization, an increased focus on personnel (both political executives and career civil servants), an increased use of presidential staff in oversight and implementation capacities, and budgeting techniques such as planned program budgeting systems, management by objectives, and zero base budgeting.

Presidents have used these management techniques to obtain

centralized control over policy implementation. "Management" refers to the manner in which choices are accomplished through policy implementation—which differs from political choice.[5] Thus, management is an important means employed by presidents to increase their political power.

As Myron Q. Hale suggests, policy implementation is an important, if often neglected, aspect of presidential power.[6] Although a president may control the decision-making process, it is difficult to say he has a great deal of power if he is unable to turn policy choices into political outcomes. According to Hale, presidents have come to realize that other political elites have the ability to limit presidential control of the bureaucracy.

Since policy is implemented primarily by a complex system of administrative agencies with some independent authority and power within the executive branch, some presidential choices are conveyed in foreign policy statements and directives which are often so vague as to leave political and bureaucratic elites free to continue behaving as they have in the past. But presidents have seen the need for stronger policy elites to super-impose presidential policy objectives on the alliance of economic elites out of government and policy elites in government agencies.[7]

Along with the realization has come a more active role for the president as manager.

PRESIDENTIAL POWER

Presidential scholars generally have not dealt with policy implementation when considering presidential power. Rather, they have focused on decision making and thus ignored an important aspect of power. In addition, scholars neglect or blur the important distinction that can be made among power, influence, and authority. This is significant because it obscures rather than clarifies the origin of and justification for presidential management.

There are three theories of presidential power. The role or heroic theory of presidential power is best expressed in the work of Edward S. Corwin, *The President: Office and Powers*, and Clinton Rossiter, *The American Presidency*. Both suggest that presidential power stems from presidential roles. Corwin elaborates upon the president's "legitimate" roles—those based upon the Constitution and long, customary practice and usage: chief of state, chief executive, commander-in-chief, and chief legislator. To these, Rossiter adds the "extra-constitutional" roles of party chief, voice of the people, protector of the peace, manager of prosperity, and world leader or leader of the coalition of free nations. For Rossiter, power is a commodity that is equal to the sum of presidential roles. In a normative sense, he feels the president needs power commensurate with presidential roles. This theory is representative of a period in which the administrative side of the presidency was not well recognized. While few will dispute that the Constitution and society assign specific roles to the president, to focus entirely on these roles misses many important aspects of the presidency. As Hale demonstrates, by concentrating on presidential roles, Rossiter and Corwin lose sight of the relationship of roles to power, purpose, and policy goals, to which implementation should be added.[8]

The second and perhaps best-known theory of presidential power is Richard Neustadt's skill or bank account theory. Neustadt argues that presidential power is personal influence—an argument that led to his famous axiom that presidential power is the ability to persuade.[9] For Neustadt, the sources of presidential power are the president's vantage point (his bargaining advantage), his professional reputation (based on the expectations of the Washington community), and his public prestige (how the Washington community thinks the public perceives the president and his actions). Power becomes a commodity that can be increased through the right decision and spent through the wrong decision. Therefore, each decision becomes a risk of presidential power, in which the result will impact the sum total of presidential power.

One of the finer points of Neustadt's analysis in his recognition of the reciprocal nature of power—that the president has power only if he is able to gain the action that he desires from other political elites. What is problematic about Neustadt's view is that it applies mainly to the decision-making process; administration and policy implementation are removed from a central consideration of presidential power. Another problem is that in making power synonymous with personal influence, Neustadt neglects other important sources of presidential influence, inter alia, the constitutional roles of the president and presidential authority.[10]

A third theory of presidential power is crisis leadership or pre-rogative power. This theory is based on John Locke's prerogatives—in times of emergency and crisis, the president can expand his powers beyond his constitutional authority and can gain control of decision making, if not the national agenda. Then, during times of "normalcy," presidential power should contract to its former boundaries. This theory is based on the commander-in-chief clause of the Constitution, the "elastic block" that can be expanded in times of presidential need. As with the two other theories of presidential power, decision making is the main focus of this analysis, even though the prerogative theory by definition is applicable only to special cases—decision making in times of crisis. This theory fails to explain not only the administrative side of presidential power but also "everyday" decisions.

Each of the three theories of presidential power leads to a concept of presidential power embodied only in the concrete decisions that presidents make and the activity bearing directly on that process. Such a concept of political power ignores the authority's origin in political and economic institutions and underplays the importance of political values, personality, and class interests, and the exercise of influence and political power by other political elites. Clearly, if presidential power is to be more applicable to the study of presidential management, a more comprehensive theory of presidential influence and power is needed.

ANOTHER VIEW OF PRESIDENTIAL POWER

In order to develop the relationship between presidential power and management, it is necessary to demonstrate that presidential influence and the constitutional position of the president do not include the concept of presidential management or the control of policy implementation. Clarifying the relation of power and management requires defining the sources of presidential influence, a task that the three theories of presidential power discussed above do only tangentially.

Myron Q. Hale makes necessary distinctions among power, influence, and authority in order to determine the sources of presidential power. According to Hale, "influence" is the encompassing term among these concepts. Influence refers chiefly to the president's ability to affect the behavior of other policy elites in and out of government.[11] Influence is based primarily on the president's institutional and personal authority.

The president's institutional authority stems mainly from his constitutional authority and the status that the presidency provides him vis-à-vis other policy elites. Article II of the Constitution provides the president with both enumerated and implied grants of authority that allow him varying degrees of participation and influence in most policy areas.

However, institutional authority also stems from the president's unique position in the political system. As the only political elite who can claim to represent the entire electorate, the president maintains the right to define the national interest. This claim provides the president with influence unmatched by any other political elite. As many authors have suggested, the president often uses this authority to his own advantage—to influence the policy process.[12]

The president's personal authority cannot be transferred and is based primarily on the president's credibility (how he is perceived by other policy elites inside and outside of government) and prestige (the public evaluation of the president). As Hale demonstrates, the president's personal authority affects his ability to influence other political elites, and a loss of personal authority can spell disaster for presidential decision making.[13]

Presidential power can be defined in part as the president's ability to implement policies regardless of the wishes or actions of other policy elites. This definition suggests that power is different from presidential influence. The difference lies in the degree of control presidents have over policy implementation. In the case of influence, the president can attempt to persuade other policy elites to implement his policies. This definition also suggests that power is a relational concept, and that presidential power does not exist in a vacuum. In order for the president to maximize his power, there must be compliant action from other elites. Therefore, a study of presidential power must consider the relationship of the power and influence of other policy elites to presidential power.[14]

There is also an internal dimension to political power that concerns a president's ability to formulate purposes and to act, to organize, and to direct activities for intended goals and results. This ability is based on personality and character and constitutes a basis of presidential leadership. Therefore, in considering presidential power, it is proper to consider leadership skills as well as presidential authority.

There are other dimensions to presidential influence besides authority and power, such as presidential beliefs and purposes, presidential actions, identification (emotional tie between citizens and the president), and social control. All of these factors affect the president's ability to influence the policy process. However, in considering the president's ability to control policy implementation, it is the weakness of constitutional authority and presidential influence that made presidents turn to management as a means of gaining control over the bureaucracy.[15]

PRESIDENTIAL INFLUENCE AND ADMINISTRATION

An investigation of the president's constitutional authority in relation to administration demonstrates just how limited presidential influence is in controlling the bureaucracy. The role of manager is not a constitutionally granted authority. As Richard M. Pious notes, "the Constitution confers neither title nor plenary authority of the chief executive on the president."[16] While the opening words of Article II of the Constitution grant to the incumbent president "the Executive Power of the United States," there is a lack of agreement about the exact meaning of these words.

In fact, there are at least two schools of thought about who has primary responsibility for administration of the federal bureaucracy. The Presidentialist view suggests that the executive is the preeminent branch of government, and the president should therefore be in control of the administrative process. The Congressionalist view argues that the intent of the Constitution is that Congress should control the bureaucracy. Presidentialists base their argument on the opening words of Article II of the Constitution and the charge that it is the president's duty to ensure proper execution of the laws. Congressionalists, on the other hand, consider the phrase granting the president the executive power of the United States to be very general, encompassing no more than the few limited powers that are specifically enumerated in the body of Article II. Moreover, Congressionalists suggest that the "faithful execution of the laws" clause should be read as an injunction against substituting presidential authority for legislative intent. This doctrine of exclusion implies that the very limited grants of authority enumerated in the Constitution indicate the framers' decision to reserve the power to superintend the departments for Congress, under the various powers of legislation, appointment, and organization granted Congress in Article I of the Constitution.[17]

However, the conflict between the president and Congress over which branch of government has the authority and responsibility for administration of the federal bureaucracy has never been resolved. In fact, the Supreme Court has recognized two independent chains of command—one presidential and one congressional. As a result of this shared chain of command, the president does not have a clear-cut grant of constitutional authority in the area of administration that can be drawn upon as a source of presidential power.[18]

In terms of particular grants of constitutional power for administration, the president is very limited. Through his power of appointment, the president can (subject to Senate approval) choose the men and women responsible for the administration of the executive departments and agencies. Even in this area, the president is limited by time and resources, if not by his constitutional authority. The president can also request the resignation of an official whose actions are inconsistent with his wishes. However, these powers scarcely provide the president with the desired type of hands-on control. In fact, it is easily argued that in constitutional terms, the president may have administrative influence, but not administrative power.

It is possible that presidents can draw upon their reserves of integrity and credibility as well as their leadership skills to assert their influence in the area of administration. As many presidential scholars have pointed out, however, the personal authority of recent presidents (with the exceptions of Gerald Ford and certainly Ronald Reagan) has not been very high. Moreover, while personal authority may give the president a degree of influence over the implementation of policy, that influence is not the same as presidential power.

Historically lacking the constitutional authority and the personal authority to control the administrative process, modern presidents have sought other means of influencing and controlling the bureaucracy. Many presidents have attempted what might be called the administrative approach. This approach stresses the twin techniques of coordination and persuasion. These presidents have used their personal authority, their superior bargaining position, and so on to extend their influence over the administrative process in a piece-meal fashion. A second approach has been to ignore domestic policy in order to concentrate on foreign policy, where the president has the advantage of a more clear-cut constitutional authority and power and fewer competing policy elites.[19] As presidents have seen their programs thwarted by the bureaucracy, they have sought greater control. Recent presidents have desired the extension and increase of presidential power in the area of administration—the ability to control policy implementation. One of the methods they have tried is presidential management and the administrative techniques that management entails.

The administrative principles that make up presidential management offer advantages to the president who is interested in increasing his power and control over the bureaucracy. Among these advantages are hierarchy, authority, and greater control over the flow of information in the executive branch. Budgeting techniques such as planned program budgeting systems and zero base budgeting are designed to overcome the decentralized nature of the budget-making process and to increase agencies' responsiveness to presidential direction.

Management techniques also tend to provide for a greater control over the flow of information into the executive office. In a highly technical society, the control of information often equates with political power.[20] The Nixon administration's management by objectives (MBO) program demonstrated this concern with increased control over the flow of information. One of the MBO program's prime goals was to increase the flow of information concerning agency budgetary objectives to the president. Nixon thought that more detailed information about agency objectives would allow him greater control over the budget process. Other presidents felt their management programs would also increase presidential control.

SUMMARY

Modern presidents have been unable to gain control over the bureaucracy and the implementation of policy programs through the use of presidential influence and authority. As domestic policy has increased in importance, presidents have sought to increase presidential power and to obtain control over policy implementation. One of the methods used is presidential management. The study of the historical evolution and current application of presidential management provides not only a greater understanding of presidential power but also the theoretical links between presidential power and management in the implementation of policy.

NOTES

1. Hugh Heclo, *A Government of Strangers* (Washington, D.C.: The Brookings Institution, 1977), p. 21.

2. R. G. H. Sin, "The Craft of Power," quoted in William J. Lanouette, "Subverting the Subterraneans," *National Journal*, vol. 11 (May 5, 1976), p. 44.

3. As shown in Heclo's *A Government of Strangers* (pp. 100-104), 77 percent of career civil servants have more than ten years' tenure, which allows them to outlast the tenure of even a two-term president.

4. For example, Joel D. Aberbach and Bert A. Rockman in "Clashing Beliefs Within the Executive Branch," *American Political Science Review*, vol. 70 (June 1976), pp. 456-468, demonstrate that a large portion of the bureaucracy was indeed ideologically opposed to the Nixon administration's objectives in domestic politics. In addition, David A. Caputo and Richard L. Cole, "Presidential Control of the Senior Civil Service: Assessing the Strategies of the Nixon Years," *American Political Science Review*, vol. 73 (June 1979), pp. 399–414, suggest that with a concerted effort, Nixon was able to change this ideological orientation.

5. Richard Rose, *Managing Presidential Objectives* (New York: Free Press, 1976), p. 15.

6. The material on presidential power is borrowed frequently and heavily from Myron Q. Hale, "Presidential Influence, Authority, and Power and Economic Policy," in Dalmas H. Nelson and Richard L. Sklar, *Toward a Humanistic Science of Politics: Essays in Honor of Francis Dunham Woarmuth* (New York: University Press of America, 1983), pp. 399-437.

7. Ibid., p. 423.

8. Ibid., pp. 403-404.

9. Richard Neustadt, *Presidential Power* (New York: John Wiley, 1960), pp. 31-34.

10. Hale, "Presidential Influence," p. 406.

11. Ibid., pp. 410-411.

12. Among the authors who point this out, see Arthur M. Schlesinger, Jr.,

The Imperial Presidency (New York: Houghton Mifflin, 1973); Thomas E. Cronin, *The State of the Presidency* (Boston: Little, Brown, 1975), chap. 2; James MacGregor Burns, *Presidential Government* (Boston: Houghton Mifflin, 1973), section II; and William F. Mullen, *Presidential Power and Politics* (New York: St. Martin's Press, 1976), chap. 2.

13. Hale, "Presidential Influence," p. 412.

14. As Hale suggests in ibid., p. 411, the main source of presidential power is the president's institutional authority. Therefore, as the institutional authority of the presidency increases or decreases, so does presidential power.

15. It is important to note that in the sense in which the term is being used, the president's personal authority is directly related to presidential skills. Obviously, the president's credibility and public prestige are going to affect his leadership skills, as are his ability to organize materials, time, and individuals. For a discussion of what bureaucratic elites perceive as important leadership skills in regard to the president, see Ross Clayton and William Lammers, "Presidential Leadership Reconsidered: Contemporary View of Top Federal Officials," *Presidential Studies Quarterly*, vol. 8 (Winter, 1978), pp. 237-244.

16. Richard M. Pious, *The American Presidency* (New York: Basic Books, 1979), p. 213.

17. An excellent discussion of this point can be found in ibid., chapter 1.

18. This dispute over administrative authority reflects the age-old problem of democratic theory—between centralized responsibility for administration and a pluralistic notion of government; in other words, the essential disagreement between Hamilton and Madison as shown in Alexander Hamilton, James Madison, John Jay, *The Federalist Papers* (New York: New American Library, 1961). Hamilton argued that the preeminent branch of government was the executive, and that it was only through the centralization of administrative regulation and operating efficiency that the liberty of the individual could be protected. According to Hamilton, a pluralistic decision-making structure concealed many faults in that it would destroy the concept of democratic responsibility and weaken the power of informed public opinion. Madison, on the other hand, argued that making the individual secure from the arbitrary actions of a tyrannical majority was the ultimate goal of justice. In Madison's view, it was the legislative branch of government that emerged as the supreme coordinator of conflicting interests, and justice was realized in direct proportion to the extent to which conflicting interests could be accomplished through commonality.

19. James Fallows, "The Passionless Presidency," *The Atlantic*, vol. 244 (May 1979), p. 40, describes the impact of foreign affairs on Carter in the following manner: After "the trips on fabulous Air Force One, the flour-

ishes, twenty-one gun salutes, and cheering multitudes along the motor-
cade routes, returning from a triumphal journey to Nigeria or Germany,
his eyes would noticeably glaze as he forced himself to talk about the reorganization of Commerce."

20. Among the most prominent authors to make this point is Jean-Jacques
Salomon in *Science and Politics* (Cambridge: MIT Press, 1973).

2
The Origins of Presidential Management

Presidential management of the bureaucracy is not only a current governmental problem but one that has specific roots in the past. Historically, there have been several environmental factors crucial to the development of presidential management. Among the most important were the major social, economic, and political upheavals of the twentieth century. These factors simultaneously gave rise to a rapid growth in the federal bureaucracy and an expanded role for the president in managing the bureaucracy. The intellectual tradition of presidential management, based primarily on the public administration literature, suggested the importance of executive management on the national level and then attempted to provide the executive with management tools. When considered together, the expanding role of government and the public administration literature demonstrate the origins and limitations of the movement toward presidential management.

SOCIAL, ECONOMIC, AND POLITICAL FORCES

A variety of social, economic, and political forces came together during the administrations of President Franklin Roosevelt to fundamentally change the relationship between the president and the bureaucracy.[1] Dwight Waldo maintains that several forces affected the growth and development of intellectual thought on the structure of the federal bureaucracy: the closing of the frontier and the waste of natural resources, the growth of tremendous wealth and the rise of the business empire, the corporate revolution and the evolution of new corporate forms, urbanization, the peculiar nature of the American constitutional and political system, the second phase of the Industrial Revolution, the increase in specialization, the Great Wars, and the Great Depression.[2] All of these factors were important, but it is clear that the impact of the depression and World Wars I and II were the primary causes of the emergence of presidential management.

When Roosevelt assumed office on March 2, 1933, the United States and the capitalist world were undoubtedly facing an economic crisis of overwhelming proportions. The gross national product had been cut in half; nearly a quarter of the work force was unemployed; many Americans were nearly starving; and business profits were negative for the second year in a row.[3] Clearly, the state of the economy and the political climate called for more than politics as usual—politics that President Herbert Hoover seemed unable or unwilling to provide.

Historians differ as to whether the changes brought about during Roosevelt's administrations were *revolutionary* in the sense that they radically changed existing economic and political relationships, or *evolutionary* in that the massive changes that occurred were designed to support existing economic and political institutions. However, there can be little doubt that Roosevelt's approach was different and that it radically changed the role of the president and the federal bureaucracy in American society.[4]

Otis L. Graham suggests that the Roosevelt administrations attempted to fundamentally alter the economy through political means, with the federal government setting up permanent instruments of collective control in order to balance purchasing power with productivity.[5] While Graham probably overstates the case in terms of the intention and permanence of Roosevelt's designs, his description of Roosevelt's actions is accurate. Graham demonstrates that the programs Roosevelt administered made an effort to provide relief to those who needed it and to manage parts of the economy that had severe structural flaws (such as land, population, transportation, energy, and incomes and credit policies). These programs had considerable impact on presidential/bureaucratic relations. The emergency relief and independent regulatory agencies added considerably to the size of the federal bureaucracy. One has only to think of the numerous "alphabet" agencies—National Recovery Administration (NRA); Works Progress Administration (WPA); Agricultural Adjustment Administration (AAA), and so on to realize the magnitude of the federal bureaucracy's growth during the Roosevelt years. Tables 1 and 2 demonstrate this bureaucratic expansion. They compare the expansion from 1920 to 1930 with that from 1930 to 1940 in terms of growth in civilian employees and governmental expenditures.

Although the agencies created during the Roosevelt administrations helped to make greater control of the economy and other private sectors of American life possible, they also made the coordination and control of the executive branch more difficult. This difficulty resulted in two major types of management reform in the Roosevelt administrations, both stemming from the recommendations of the President's Commission on Administrative Management,

Table 1
Federal Civilian Employees

1920s	1930s
1920 – 655,265	1930 – 601,319
1925 – 533,045	1935 – 780,582
1930 – 601,319	1940 – 1,042,420

Table 2
Government Expenditures (thousands of dollars)

1920s	1930s
1920 – 6,357,677	1930 – 3,320,211
1925 – 2,923,762	1935 – 6,497,008
1930 – 3,320,211	1940 – 9,055,269

also called the Brownlow Committee. Reorganization was proposed as a means of integrating the emergency relief agencies into the existing structure of the executive branch, and of providing order and control over the "patchwork quilt" nature of the federal bureaucracy.[6]

Staffing, the second reform, was an attempt to cultivate an institutional capacity to recognize social problems, develop policy responses, and coordinate policy at the center of the executive branch. In 1933, Roosevelt was assisted in the White House by a cook, a butler, a switchboard operator, several guards, a handful of secretaries, and two southern newspapermen who served as aides. There was no Executive Office of the President and no economic or technical staff. The Brownlow reforms attempted to provide the president with the staff necessary to develop an institutional capacity for management.

Another major influence on presidential/bureaucratic relations during the past half-century were the two world wars. Although World War II had a greater impact because of the size of the undertaking, World War I provided an important context for the conduct of World War II, as well as for many of the other policy decisions made by the Roosevelt administrations. At the time, World War I represented the federal government's most massive intrusion into the private sectors of American society. For approximately sixteen months, the government commanded the major economic and manpower resources of the country; recruited, trained, and supplied an expeditionary army; and trained the allied forces.[7] The following quotation describes the extent of the government involvement.

The Shipping Board took control of all shipping over 2500 tons and established government shipyards to increase the size of the merchant fleet. The Railroad Administration operated the nation's railroads as a unit, breaking through a traffic bottleneck that had existed in early 1917 as private roads carrying the orders of uncoordinated federal agencies became hopelessly snarled. The Selective Service moved 4 million young men (16 percent of the male labor force) into the armed services, where they were housed, trained, and deployed at stations around the country and in France. The Fuel Administration instituted coal rationing and rationalized coal marketing to mimimize crosshauls. The Committee on Public Information manipulated public opinion. The War Finance Corporation lent money to munitions manufacturers. The Capital Issues Committee passed on new securities.[8]

However, the greatest impact of the war mobilization was psychological rather than physical. Although the government was involved in directing many private sector activities, the myth of government direction and control was greater than the reality. The impact of the war experience was particularly strong on policy-making elites. As Otis L. Graham suggests, "For the lawyers, businessmen, and economists, social workers, statisticians, engineers, and others who staffed the bustling mobilization agencies, World War I was a revelation in the advantages of an economy managed through government/business cooperation."[9]

The government's role during World War II was even larger. Graham describes the manner in which the government conduct of the war met the criteria of a planned society.

The Selective Service System and War Manpower Commission were a giant manpower agency, not only sending 10 million citizens into the war theaters abroad but deciding toward the end of the war whether to keep people in farming or dentistry or electronics, draft them, or allow them to migrate to jobs in defense plants. There were appropriate agencies for all these controls, and a central coordinating bureau at the apex. The essentials of planning were all there—policy goals, government manipulation of the basic social sectors, appropriate institutional machinery for coordination.[10]

It was a form of planning that made few friends and, in the long run, hurt as well as helped the cause of presidential management. Many people remembered the experience not in terms of the successful conduct of the war but rather for inefficient management and the bureaucratic expansion into everyday life. It was a type of action that could be accepted in a wartime emergency, but not in a time of peace.

INTELLECTUAL THOUGHT AND PRESIDENTIAL MANAGEMENT

Reform

In addition to the material forces, there were also considerable intellectual forces behind the emergence of presidential management. For more than fifty years prior to Franklin Roosevelt's administrations, progressive intellectuals such as Lester Frank Ward, Richard T. Ely, John Dewey, Walter Lippmann, Herbert Croly, and Charles Van Hise had taught the necessity of public intervention as a guide to modern social evolution in a highly industrialized nation. They believed, says Dwight Waldo,

that democracy must rethink its positions and remold its institutions, particularly it must create a strong right arm for the state in the form of an efficient bureaucracy. They knew that the way to realize a purpose is not to leave it to chance, and that the future must be given shape from above.[11]

Although the reformist tradition was organized at the local level to deal with corruption and waste in state and local governments, many of the movement's basic propositions were easily adapted to the national level. Vincent Ostrum identifies the following propositions of the Reformist Era:

1. There will always be a single dominant center of power in any system of government, and the government of a society will be controlled by that single center of power.

2. The more power is divided, the more irresponsible it becomes; or alternatively, the more power is unified and directed from a single center, the more responsible it will become.

3. The structure of a constitution defines and determines the composition of that center of power and establishes the political structure relative to the enactment of law and the control of administration. Every system of democratic government will exalt the people's representative to a position of absolute sovereignty.

4. The field of politics sets the task of administration, but the field of administration lies outside the proper sphere of politics.

5. All modern governments will have a strong structural similarity insofar as administrative functions are concerned.

6. Perfection in the hierarchical ordering of a professionally trained public service provides the structural conditions necessary for "good" administration.

7. Perfection in the hierarchical organization will maximize efficiency as measured by the least cost expended in money and effort.

8. Perfection of "good" administration as above defined is a necessary con-
dition for the modernity in human civilization and for the advancement
of human welfare.[12]

In addition to these propositions, the reform tradition expressed
an overwhelming belief in progress as defined in material terms, in
the validity of science as the "engine" of progress, and in executive
management as the key to responsibility as well as efficiency.[13] As
a body of thought and techniques, the reform movement can be
viewed as an effort to preserve the essential parts of the American
heritage, conceived and developed under comparatively simple rural conditions, possessed by a large industrial nation, itself in an
international situation of increasing complexity.[14]

The reform movement (particularly in public administration) is
of utmost importance for the trend toward presidential management. The movement's intellectual and practical aspects set the stage
for the basic reforms of the Roosevelt administrations. Many of the
people responsible for developing these reforms were themselves
part of the reform movement. However, the importance of the reform movement's impact that lasted long beyond the Roosevelt administrations is in the tradition of management that its basic principles support. Many of the reform movement's propositions provide
the framework for current management techniques.[15]

Public Administration

The intellectual tradition of public administration is closely linked
to the development of presidential management. Not only have public
administration concepts proven useful in the application of presidential management but various public administration scholars have
directly participated in the reforms that played an essential role in
the development of presidential management. In addition, public
administrationists have provided useful rationales for the expansion
of presidential power vis-à-vis the federal bureaucracy.

Many people mark the inception of public administration as a
discipline with the publication of Woodrow Wilson's seminal article, "The Study of Public Administration." However, the origins of
the discipline can be found many years earlier, in the growing
awareness that the popular democracy of the Jacksonian era con-

tained serious problems for a nation that was becoming a modern industrial society.[16] Among these problems was the sense of a lack of direction and leadership, which was viewed as detrimental to the interests of the established elite. Out of these concerns grew the two major approaches to the public administration movement. One approach emphasized method and was characterized by a search for precise technical systems for identifying problems and seeking their solutions. The other approach emphasized the need for a continuously expanding elite to provide knowledge and rationale for social management. These two approaches underlie public administration and presidential management.

The history of public administration as an academic area can be categorized into four district paradigms.[17] The first was the Politics/Administration Dichotomy (1900 to 1925). This paradigm began with Woodrow Wilson's recognition of the differences between the worlds of politics and administration. Frank Goodnow, in *Politics and Administration*, and Leonard White, in *Introduction to the Study of Administration*, thoroughly develop the basic distinctions by relating the politics/administration dichotomy to a corresponding value/fact dichotomy. The world of politics included the irrational factors of political life (participation, representation, public opinion, and political choice). The world of administration, on the other hand, represented the elements of fact and science. Goodnow and White argue that government could be divided into two parts—decision and execution—and that execution (administration) could be made into a science. Therefore, public administration theory simultaneously divorced politics from administration and created the confines of its own study. Public administrationists would study the executive branch, particularly the implementation of policy, while the study of policy-making was to be left to political scientists.

The second part of this paradigm was the scientific management movement. Based upon the works of Frederick Taylor, this movement's major propositions fit well with those of the early public administrationists. Wallace S. Sayre identifies the following doctrines of the scientific management movement:

1. The politics/administration dichotomy was assumed both as a self-evident truth and as a desirable goal; administration was perceived as a self-contained world of its own, with its own rules, values, and methods.

2. Organization theory was stated in "scientific management" terms; that is, it was seen largely as a problem in organization technology—the necessities of hierarchy, the uses of staff agencies, a limited span of control, subdivision of work by such scientific principles as purpose, process, place, or clientele.

3. The executive budget was emphasized as an instrument of rationality, coordination, planning, and control.

4. Personnel management was stressed as an additional element of rationality (jobs were to be described "scientifically" and employees were to be selected, paid, and advanced by "scientific methods").

5. A neutral or impartial career service was required to ensure competence, expertise, and rationality.

6. A body of administrative law was needed to prescribe standards of due process in administrative conduct.[18]

The principles of the scientific management movement in addition to the reform movement continue to exert an influence on presidential management methods.

A second paradigm of public administration was the Principles of Public Administration (1925 to 1940). This paradigm suggested that there are distinct administrative principles that can be identified and applied to the management of large-scale organizations. To the literature of this paradigm, Luther Gulick contributed the principles of management: planning, organizing, staffing, directing, coordinating, reporting, and budgeting, otherwise recognized by its acronym—POSDCORB. According to Gulick, these are the basic principles of administration that underlie the successful direction of any organization, and the techniques that the successful administrator must employ.[19]

In many ways, this period represented the high-water mark of public administration. At the time, there was a consensus in the field about the object and method of administrative research. The discipline as a whole was well respected academically, and administrative scholars had the ears of presidents and influence in the direction of administration policy on the national level. And well they might, for the logic of their research created the need for their expertise. The public administration literature suggests that a group of individuals should be in charge of the management of public policy. To argue that policy should be managed implies the need for professional managers, and the public administration discipline was training such a group.

As Allen Schick suggests, the politics/administration dichotomy, rather than separating politics and administration, really offered a framework for bringing them together.[20] The dichotomy provided for the ascendancy of the administrative over the political, efficiency over representation, and rationality over self-interest. The subservience of politics to administration furnished a theoretical basis and practical guidance for admitting administrative values into the political sphere. The reformers could use the same arguments in favor of fewer elected officials or fewer units of government to justify fewer administrative agencies. Thus, the literature created a false separation between politics and administration, which served as the dominant political theory guiding both public administration and politics during this period. This theory called for an administrative elite who would serve the existing economic and social elite rather than replace them. On the national level, the chief executive's new role would be to lead and manage this elite.

The apex of this public administration paradigm can best be marked by the Bronlow Committee Reports of 1937. Afterward came a period of reflection and questioning of the discipline's basic postulations (The Challenge, 1938–1947). Criticism was directed toward three basic tenets of the paradigm. First, Dwight Waldo and Robert Dahl questioned the discipline's ability to adopt a neutral, value-free, "scientific" position.[21] They suggested that public administration should not be value free and neutral (even if in fact it could be—a position that Waldo rejects). They argued that the study of administration must be aimed at political ends, toward which the administrative process should be directed. Waldo, for example, argued that it is not enough to adopt the concept of efficiency as a neutral, value-free goal of administration. Rather, the question should be of efficiency to what ends, of what type, and to benefit whom.

Second, the politics/administration dichotomy was increasingly challenged. Herbert Simon argued that the distinctions between politics and administration were artificial and that political decisions were an integral part of the administrative process.[22] This criticism grew out of the World War II experience of many public administration scholars. Some of these scholars served in the federal government in an administrative capacity, and it was clear that the politics/administration dichotomy did not adequately reflect their bureaucratic experience.

Third, there was an almost total rejection of the principles of administration within the discipline itself. Simon demonstrated that the principles of administration were not really principles at all but merely proverbs based on intuition rather than on scientific observation. Moreover, Simon showed that the principles were not even consistent, and in fact were often contradictory. These criticisms still have not been answered. It is safe to say that since the critical analysis of the 1940s, public administration has lacked the self-confidence and coherence of the period between the wars and that no new orthodoxy has arisen to replace the principles of public administration.

The early 1950s began a decline in intellectual prestige for the discipline. It also marked a period of search for a new orthodoxy that has not yet been found. This search culminated in a fourth paradigm of public administration: Public Administration as Administrative Science. "Administrative science" is used here as a catchall term for studies in organization theory and management science. In fact, administrative science may not even be a paradigm; as Nicholas Henry suggests, it provides a focus for study, but not a locus.[23] This paradigm offered techniques (often highly sophisticated) that required a great deal of expertise and training, but it failed to provide the institutional setting in which the expertise should be applied.

During these years, many changes occurred in public administration. The "new public administration" emerged, which challenged the elitist tendencies of the old guard. This new administration argued that public administration should be more socially conscious and should actively attempt to bring the unrepresented into the administrative process. Although the new public administration delivered a successful intellectual challenge to the dogmatism of the discipline, it has been less successful in finding a method for the study and practice of administration.

Perhaps more germane to this research is the rise of the generic school of public administration. The generic approach argues that the core of administrative activities is the same in public and nonpublic organizations, and while "public" adds something to the administrative enterprise, it is more productive for research and training to concentrate on the common elements of administrative activities.[24] The generic approach's popularity is due in part to the feeling that standard public administration courses do not equip students with the competence necessary for the administration of large-scale organizations. The judgment is that the conventional curriculum has ceased being a wellspring of administrative innovation; it has been oriented to basic personnel, budgeting, and administrative practices and does not give adequate attention to modern analytic and informational techniques. In contrast, the generic schools provide a heavy dose of problem solving, decisional strategy, and business school staples such as management by objectives and training in the use of statistics and data.

Concurrent with the rise of the generic school of public administration, many business schools (particularly the Harvard Business School) have become actively involved in the conduct of public sector administration. Their students have taken government jobs, and their faculties have taken government grants and contracts. Moreover, management consulting firms began selling their wares to public as well as private clients. The business schools are directly responsible for introducing management techniques such as planned program budgeting systems, management by objectives, and zero base budgeting into the federal government.

Many of the management techniques of the generic approach to public administration are based on the same concepts as the early principles of public administration. While it might be felt that the inadequacy of public administration research and thought is responsible for the generic approach to the study of public administration, it cannot be said that the generic approach overcomes the normative criticisms cited earlier. There is little consideration of the normative purposes of administration. Instead, the emphasis has been on a pragmatic approach to administration.

SUMMARY

The consideration of various historical factors related to the development of presidential management leads to several important conclusions. In the Roosevelt administrations, presidential management emerged in conjunction with important social, economic, and political changes in the country, which brought about an expanding role for the president and the federal bureaucracy in the private sectors of American life. Along with this expanded role came an equal growth in both the responsibilities and size of the executive departments. Thus, policy became more difficult to implement, and presidents complained of their inability to control the executive branch.

Concurrent with the growth of the executive branch was the growth of public administration, which offered solutions to the developing problems. At the same time, the principles that were being accepted and applied in the federal government were rejected by public administrationists. However, the principles continue to be applied at the national level. As David R. Beam maintains, "public administration is alive and well in the White House."[25] Is this because the principles provide effective management and increase presidential influence in the administration of policy, or because the alternatives presidents face are inaction and lack of influence?

NOTES

1. A survey of the literature on management in Franklin Roosevelt's administration indicates that it would not be improper to suggest that presidential management really starts with the Roosevelt administration.

2. Dwight Waldo, *The Administrative State* (New York: Ronald Press, 1948), p. 3.

3. Otis L. Graham, *Toward a Planned Society* (New York: Oxford University Press, 1976), pp. 3-4.

4. For a revisionist perspective on the Roosevelt administration, see Paul K. Conlin, *FDR and the Origins of the Welfare State* (New York: Thomas Y. Crowell, 1967).

5. Graham, *Toward a Planned Society*, chap. 1.

6. Richard Polenberg, *Reorganizing Roosevelt's Government* (Cambridge: Harvard University Press, 1966), p. 5. Actually, the phrase "patchwork quilt of government" can be attributed to Hoover, who also recognized the need for reorganizing the executive branch. However, because of Hoover's lame-duck status, Congress refused to grant him authority to reorganize the executive branch.

7. Graham, *Toward a Planned Society*, p. 59.

8. Ibid.

9. Ibid., p. 13.

10. Ibid., p. 73.

11. Waldo, *The Administrative State*, p. 17.

12. Vincent Ostrum, *The Intellectual Crisis in American Public Administration* (University, Ala.: University of Alabama Press, 1973), p. 28.

13. Dwight Waldo, "Public Administration," *International Encyclopedia of the Social Sciences*, vol. 13 (New York: Macmillan and Free Press, 1948), p. 146.

14. Ibid.

15. Barry Dean Karl, "Public Administration and American History," *Public Administration Review*, vol. 36 (1976), p. 490.

16. Waldo, "Public Administration," p. 147.

17. These paradigms of public adminstration were borrowed from Nicholas Henry, *Public Administration and Public Affairs* (Englewood Cliffs, N.J.: Prentice-Hall, 1975), chap. 1.

18. Wallace S. Sayre, "Premises of Public Administration," *Public Administration Review*, vol. 8 (1948), p. 102.

19. Luther Gulick, *Papers on the Science of Administration* (New York: Institute of Public Administration, 1937).

20. Allen Schick, "The Trauma of Politics: Public Administration in the Sixties," in Frederick Mosher, *American Public Administration: Past, Present, Future* (University, Ala.: University of Alabama Press, 1974).

21. Waldo, "Public Administration," p. 148.

22. Herbert Simon, *Administrative Behavior* (New York: Macmillan, 1957).

23. Henry, *Public Administration and Public Affairs*, p. 15.

24. Schick, "The Trauma of Politics," p. 84.

25. David R. Beam, "Public Administration is Alive and Well in the White House," *Public Administration Review*, vol. 38 (1978), p. 72.

3
The History of Management Techniques

Presidents have used a variety of management techniques in attempting to gain control over the bureaucracy: reorganization, manipulation of personnel, and budgeting.[1] Even though there are similarities in their application, each of the management techniques has had a unique historical development.

REORGANIZATION

Reorganization is one of the earliest and most widely used administrative techniques for presidential management.[2] Since Franklin D. Roosevelt's administration, presidents have used reorganization as a means to control policy implementation in the executive branch.[3] Between 1939 and 1973, there were 105 reorganization plans submitted to Congress. Of these plans, only 23 were disapproved. President Harry S Truman gained 32 of 48 reorganization plans; President Dwight D. Eisenhower 14 of 17; President John F. Kennedy, 6 of 10; President Lyndon B. Johnson, 17 of 17; and President Richard M. Nixon, 3 of 3.[4] Obviously, presidents have not only been prolific in proposing reorganization plans, but have also been successful in getting them through Congress.

The president was first given the authority to reorganize the executive branch under the Legislative Appropriations Act of 1932.[5] The features of the original act have been incorporated into subse-

quent reorganizations. These normally provide that presidential reorganization acts go into effect if neither chamber of Congress dis-
approves by resolution, within a specific period of usually sixty days.
If the president wants to create new departments or agencies or to
increase or decrease their authority, legislative proposals must be
submitted to Congress.

In 1973, as part of the general reaction to Watergate, Congress
broke with tradition and refused to extend reorganization authority
to a Republican president. In 1977, with the election of a Democratic president committed to major reorganization, the Democratic
Congress passed a new organization act. It permitted the president
to submit plans for individual departments and agencies but didn't
allow for any omnibus plans for complete executive branch reorganizations. Unlike earlier versions, the 1977 act withheld permis-
sion for creating or abolishing agencies or terminating any statutory
functions.

Prior to Franklin Roosevelt's administration, there had been several investigations into the possibility of reorganizations to increase
management. In the thirty years following the Civil War, Congress
sponsored four investigations into departmental management. In each
case, the objective was to increase economy through management
methods, and the underlying assumption was that the legislature
was responsible for the administrative system.[6] Of these attempts,
the Dockrell Commission (1893) was perhaps the most successful.
Also of consequence was the Keep Commission, appointed by
Theodore Roosevelt in 1905 to study administrative procedures,
symbolizing the transfer of responsibility for administrative reform
from the legislative to the executive branch.

An important facet of Franklin Roosevelt's reorganization proposals was a change in the objective of reorganization. Earlier presidents considered reorganization as a means for decreasing expenditures. Under Roosevelt, the primary objective became improved
management rather than economy.[7] The emphasis was on making
the bureaucracy more responsive to the president rather than on
saving money.

Franklin Roosevelt's administration faced a great need for improved management. Prior to the 1930s, there was a growing
awareness that the federal bureaucracy was becoming difficult to

manage, but Roosevelt's response to the Depression only increased the management problem. The main thrust of the Roosevelt management style was to create new, independent agencies to administer presidential programs rather than to work through existing departments and agencies.[8] As a short-term management approach, it was felt that such efforts provided the president with greater control over his emergency relief programs. In the long term, however, effective management required that these programs and agencies be integrated into the existing structure of the executive branch. Reorganization became a means for merging these agencies with the existing bureaucracy and for achieving effective coordination of domestic policy. On March 22, 1936, Franklin Roosevelt appointed the President's Commission on Administrative Management (or the Brownlow Committee) to study means of increasing policy coordination through the consolidation of agencies, and to seek ways to enhance the president's control over career civil servants who were dragging their feet on New Deal programs. Louis Brownlow, Charles Merriam, and Luther Gulick were members of the committee. As the following quotation suggests, the makeup of the committee presaged its basic recommendations and the resulting presidential acceptance.

Brownlow, a lifelong Democrat, shared with Roosevelt a common bond of association with Woodrow Wilson. Merriam, formerly a progressive Republican, had come to support the New Deal not only because it offered a chance to fulfill the program of the New Nationalism, but because it gave power to old Bull Moose like his good friend Harold Ickes. Merriam was always "Uncle Charley" to both Roosevelt and Ickes. Luther Gulick too had deserted the Republican party by 1933. All three men sympathized with the New Deal, ardently admired the President and valued his friendship. Their political views closely corresponded to those of the President. They were convinced that the American Presidency represented the most reliable bulwark against the tide of totalitarianism, that it was the institution around and behind which Democrats might rally to repel the enemy. They were dismayed by the expansion of European fascism and the violence that accompanied it. To demonstrate freedom and efficiency were linked, that democratic societies could act with promptness and vigor, the President must be given authority to match his responsibility. Congress should concentrate on setting down general principles; the President should be free to execute the laws and administer the government.[9]

The Brownlow Committee sought to create a presidency that would contain the efficiency and technological skills required in a modern industrial society, at the same time maintaining the American public's freedom to choose the president. Toward these ends, the committee proposed the following reforms.

1. Expand the White House staff so that the president may have a sufficient group of able assistants in his own office to keep closer and easier touch with the widespread affairs of administration and to make quicker the clearance of the knowledge needed for executive decision.

2. Strengthen and develop the managerial agencies of the government, particularly those dealing with the budget and efficiency research, with personnel and planning as management arms of the chief executive.

3. Extend the merit system upward, outward, and downward to cover all nonpolicy determining posts; reorganize the civil service system as part of management under a single responsible administrator; create a citizen board to serve as the watchdog of the merit system and to increase the salaries of key posts throughout the service so that the government may attract and hold career service men and women of ability and character.

4. Overhaul the 100 independent agencies, administrations, authorities, boards, and commissions, and place them by executive order within one or the other of the following twelve major executive departments: State, Treasury, War, Justice, Post Office, Navy, Conservation, Agriculture, Commerce, Labor, Social Welfare, and Public Works. Place upon the executive continuing responsibility for the maintenance of effective organization.

5. Establish accountability of the executive to Congress by providing a genuine postaudit of all fiscal transactions by an auditor general, and restore to the executive complete responsibility for accounts and current transactions.[10]

Roosevelt had limited success in turning these recommendations into actual reorganization plans and in getting them through Congress. When he first proposed the Reorganization Act of 1938, it contained all of the committee recommendations. However, there were many opponents of the legislation, all of whom argued that the reforms granted the president too much power. In 1938, these opponents were successful in defeating the legislation. In 1939,

Roosevelt proposed a second reorganization plan that was much less comprehensive and that omitted many of the more controversial parts of the Brownlow Committee recommendations. The Reorganization Act of 1939 authorized the president to suggest reorganization plans subject to a veto by a majority of both houses, and to appoint six administrative assistants. The modernization of the civil service system, the renovation of accounting procedures, and the creation of new government departments were dropped from the legislation.[11] The blandness of the bill assured its passage.

Generally unsuccessful during the second term of his administration, Roosevelt had greater success in adapting the Brownlow recommendations into legislation during his third term. He received authorization to submit to Congress reorganization plans that would become effective sixty days after transmittal, unless within that time they were disapproved by a concurrent resolution passed by both houses of Congress. Presidential reorganization authority was limited in that no changes could be made in the existing names or numbers of the twelve executive departments. Congress also exempted twenty-one agencies from the presidential reorganization authority.[12] Roosevelt submitted five reorganization plans to Congress, all of which were approved. Important changes brought about by the reorganization plans included the creation of the Executive Office of the President (EOP), the transfer of the Bureau of the Budget from the Treasury Department to EOP, and the creation of three department-like organizations, under which most of the agencies set up outside the regular departments were placed—except for those specifically exempted from the Reorganization Act.

The Roosevelt administration's importance in the history of reorganization is manifold. First, it marked a shift in the objective of reorganization, from econommy to management. The emphasis on management placed the reorganization efforts in congruence with popular administrative theory, which is not surprising given the backgrounds of the Brownlow Committee members. In addition, the heavy emphasis on personnel, accounting, and budgeting were in the tradition of the early principles of public administration. The Roosevelt administration (in conjunction with the doctrines of public administration) gave credibility and acceptability to reorganization as a management tool and strengthened the president's role as administrator. This increased presidential influence over the bureaucracy by providing continuity in the president's authority to reorganize the executive branch.

A second major reorganization effort occurred with the Hoover Commission Reports of 1949 and 1953. The first Hoover Commission Report (1949) was sponsored by a legislative initiative, though President Harry S Truman was quick to endorse the idea because it allowed him to influence the makeup of the commission.[13] Originally, the reorganization's objectives were substantive in nature—to investigate programs and agencies to determine their effectiveness, and to eliminate those not serving a useful purpose. However, Truman's reelection and the active resistance of his commission members forced Hoover to turn from a substantive approach to improving management capacities in the executive branch.

If volume can be taken as an indication of effort, then it must be granted that the commission directed a great deal of effort toward their task. The commission's final report in 1949 was supported by two million words of findings delivered by twenty-three task forces.[14] The report included 124 reforms, and the commission predicted both managerial improvements and savings if their advice was taken. No doubt the commission pushed the savings aspects of their report further than the data allowed, hoping that a grateful public would support their conclusions. For example, the commission admitted that, at best, only 2 percent of the national budget could be saved by economies, and that the chief problem in American government was not waste but division, diffusion, weakened management, and inadequate authority.[15]

The Hoover Commission's principal thrust was to follow one of the primary dicta of public administration: to attempt to organize the bureaucracy by major purpose groupings, in order to eliminate overlap and duplication, and to create clear lines of administrative authority and responsibility. However, because the commission wished to avoid internal and external conflict, it did not push the idea of major purpose groupings to the hilt. Instead, it nibbled. While recommending that a few agencies and programs be transferred between departments, the commission refused to tackle the problems raised by the large constituency departments, such as Labor, Agriculture, and Commerce. Moreover, the commission left twelve agencies entirely outside department boundaries, including the Tennessee Valley Authority, the Atomic Energy Commission, and the Veterans Administration. It was clear that tampering with these agencies would raise both bureaucratic and constituency opposition that the commission would rather avoid. Overlooking these problems of executive reorganization, the commission went on to make more than two hundred additional recommendations, including the abolition of certain agencies, the reduction of paperwork, and the improvement of civil service methods.[16]

The second Hoover Commission Report (1953) was organized at the request of President Dwight D. Eisenhower. In some ways, the commission reports can be seen as a throwback to an earlier era, since many of its own objectives directly contradicted the trends of the reorganization movement. For example, while the reorganization objective had shifted from economy to management, the second Hoover Commission Report was almost silent on the subject of management. Instead, it concentrated on tales of waste and expense in the federal bureaucracy. The report's most significant element was a review of government business activities, intended to determine whether they might be run more economically by private enterprise. Containing 314 recommendations for reform and backed by three million words of commentary, the commission's report, in the words of its staff directors, presented "a documented picture of sprawling and voracious bureaucracy, of monumental waste, excesses and extravagances, of red tape, confusion and disheartening frustrations, of loose management, regulatory irresponsibilities and colossal largess to special segments of the public. . . ."[17] Alas for Hoover, the opportunity for this type of reform had passed (if in fact it had ever existed); for the most part, the commission recommendations fell on deaf ears.[18]

The Hoover Commission's reorganization efforts illustrate several important points about reorganization as a management tool. First, the reports solidified the movement toward presidential management, particularly through the use of reorganization for increasing presidential control over bureaucratic processes. Second, the reports demonstrated the relationship between presidential leadership and effective management. Part of the reason for both reports' lack of success was that the presidents involved were not very interested in the conclusions. This is especially true with the report of the 1949 commission. Other than making sure that the New Deal was not revoked, Truman was simply not that interested in reorganization. Several authors have suggested that had Truman lent more weight to the commission findings, the principle of reorganization by functional groupings might have been pursued more vigorously.[19] Without presidential support, the commission did not have the political clout to combat the bureaucratic and constituency interests. Finally, the second Hoover Commission Report effectively concluded the shift in the reorganization objective from economy to efficiency through management.

A third reorganization effort of significance occurred during the Nixon administration. Nixon, like most previous presidents, appointed a council on government organization soon after his election in 1968. The council, chaired by his longtime friend and advisor Roy Ash, was known as the Ash Council.[20] The recommendations of the Ash Council were twofold. The first part, announced in 1970, dealt with the reorganization of the Executive Office of the President (EOP). The council recommended the creation of a Domestic Council in EOP for evaluating policy programs and goals and suggested that the Bureau of the Budget be reorganized to increase its management capabilities.

A year later, Nixon announced a second part to his reorganization effort, again based on the Ash Council's recommendations. In the 1971 State of the Union Address, Nixon proposed plans for regrouping major domestic cabinet departments into four super-departments: Human Resources, Community Development, Natural Resources, and Economic Affairs. His reason for the reorganization was to create a clear line of authority from the president to those responsible for implementing the primary goals of the domestic program. Nixon also appointed four super-cabinet secretaries who were responsible for the programs in the areas controlled by the super-departments.[21] Little came from this part of the Nixon reorganization effort. While some feel that Watergate was the determining factor in Nixon's abandonment of the reorganization effort, others suggest that the affected departments forced the president to modify and then abandon the reorganization effort.[22] No doubt, Nixon (because of subgovernment concerns) was under pressure from various sources to exempt the Agriculture Department from the reorganization effort. Once that exemption occurred, it was difficult to impose the plan on the rest of the bureaucracy.

Understanding the motives behind the Nixon reorganization proposals requires viewing them in the context of Nixon's antagonistic
relations with the bureaucracy. Nixon, realizing that the career civil
service had been appointed under Democratic administrations and
surmising that they would be hostile to the initiatives of a Republican administration, perceived the bureaucracy as basically hostile
to his administration's goals.[23] To this suspicion was added the more
general antagonisms that exist between any president and the bureaucracy. Together, these problems created an overwhelming need
in the Nixon administration for controlling the bureaucracy. In Nixon's view, reorganization would provide him with a degree of control over the bureaucracy. Other methods employed by the Nixon
administration included the manipulation of the career civil service
and the use of his staff and advisors as a counterbureaucracy.

Given the Nixon administration's subsequent problems, it is too
easy to evaluate the reorganization proposals solely on the merits
of the president who proposed them. However, the Nixon reorganization effort continued the tradition of extending presidential power
and influence through management techniques. In some ways, the
reorganization plans represented a creative attempt, within the confines of traditional administrative theory, to resolve several management problems. Presidents have always had difficulty in controlling
domestic agencies (much more so than their foreign policy coun-
terparts) because of the highly decentralized nature of policy decision making and implementation in those areas.[24] As a result, domestic agencies have often been relegated to a lower status within
the advisory system.[25] Nixon's strategy was to increase his control
over domestic agencies by elevating their status within the executive branch. The attempt proved to be too provocative and was
doomed to failure from the start for the very reasons that the recommendations of the first Hoover Commission failed. Without the
support of the bureaucracy itself (or at least the support of Congress), the plan would be unsuccessful.

PERSONNEL

Presidents have also relied on the manipulation of personnel as
a management technique for controlling the bureaucracy. The manipulation of personnel has taken two basic forms: the use of pres-

idential staff to control the bureaucracy and the manipulation of the career civil service. The president appoints, without the advice of the Senate, approximately sixty White House senior staff and aides. With the advice and consent of the Senate, he also appoints executive-level positions, including eight hundred or more secretaries, undersecretaries, and assistant secretaries of the departments, and the administrators and deputies for various independent agencies.[26] These political executives compose his administration and exercise the president's constitutional authority to superintend the agencies and the authority that Congress delegates to them.

The use of the White House staff in a management capacity has its origins in the Roosevelt administration, when, on the advice of the Brownlow Committee, the president was given six full-time aides. According to the committee, the staff should be the eyes and ears of the president and should "not in any way be interposed between the president and the heads of his departments; they should not be the assistants of the president in any way."[27] Their advice has not always been followed. The number of White House aides increased to 45 by the end of World War II. By the close of the Truman administration, it reached 250. The number of White House aides passed 400 under Eisenhower and got as high as 640 by the end of the Nixon administration, before it declined to 485 by the end of the Ford presidency. By July of his first term in office, Carter had 528 White House aides, of which 460 were full time, 17 were part time, and 100 were detailed from the departments and not officially listed as members of the White House office.[28]

Although all modern presidents used the presidential staff to attempt to gain control over the bureaucracy, the style in which this was accomplished has varied greatly. Franklin Roosevelt's guiding principle was that his assistants did *his* work and did not go into business for themselves. Therefore, he would not permit the White House staff to become so large that he could not supervise it himself; nor would he permit a chief of staff to do it for him. He also gave a minimum of fixed assignments, trying to create a staff of generalists. In his view, this gave him a great deal of flexibility. Roosevelt was solely concerned with congressional relations, political appointments, and cabinet-level contacts, and used his administrative assistants as his eyes and ears, with no fixed contacts, clientele, or involvements that would interfere if he decided to redeploy them. In fact, Roosevelt would often deploy several aides on the same assignment, which allowed for checks on their work and a variety of input into the decision-making process.[29] In summary, he employed his staff in such a way as to put himself at the center rather than the top of his administration. All activities flowed outward from Roosevelt, while information flowed inward.

Truman's staff organization can best be described as the opposite of Roosevelt's. While Roosevelt's staff was disorganized but powerful, Truman's was well-organized but less powerful. Moreover, Truman tended to administer the government through his cabinet rather than through powerful White House operatives.[30] Truman, was, however, innovative in shaping the White House office. The two most important staff offices in his administration were the Assistant to the President and the Special Counsel. Truman created the former (later to grow in prestige and importance, particularly in the Nixon administration) and allowed the latter to evolve into an important legislative and policy-shaping institution.[31]

The elaborate staff organization of the Eisenhower White House has been widely noted. The Eisenhower style transformed an informal group of senior assistants into an integrated structure. His staff was organized by the principles of the chain of command, and authority flowed from the president through his chief of staff (Sherman Adams) to other presidential assistants. Eisenhower continued most of the traditional staff offices developed during the Roosevelt and Truman administrations, such as Press Secretary, Congressional Relations Office, Special Counsels Office, and Appointments Secretary. In many ways, Eisenhower was responsible for the institutionalization of the basic structure of the White House staff begun by Roosevelt and Truman.

Eisenhower was also responsible for four innovations in the use of staff. First, he used the position of Assistant to the President as a chief of staff (under Sherman Adams), an administrative policy that most presidents have continued to employ. Second, he formalized the National Security Council System into a policy-making body and appointed a Special Assistant for National Security Affairs, upon whom Eisenhower drew heavily for advice. Third, he created two new staff positions—the Staff Secretary and the Secretary to the Cabinet—to systematize the flow of paperwork in the Executive Office. Finally, Eisenhower created numerous posts of Special Assistant to the President in order to bring prominent outsiders into the administration for their advice.[32]

The staff system under Eisenhower was a textbook example of the principles of staffing according to the public administration literature. He utilized the basic principles of hierarchy and span of control in organizing his staff. However, in allowing Adams so much discretion as his chief of staff, Eisenhower greatly limited his own ability to control his staff, even though this system simplified the decision-making process. The main beneficiary of the Eisenhower administration's chief of staff system seemed to be Adams, not Eisenhower. Most observers also feel that Eisenhower's system lacked flexibility and creativity, unlike Roosevelt's more pliant style of staffing.

President Kennedy, like Roosevelt, wanted to maximize his role in the conduct of his office. Therefore, Kennedy employed flexible arrangements and increased staff responsibility. In an attempt to cut back on the size of the staff, Kennedy eliminated the Staff Secretariat, the Assistant to the President, and some other related positions. He also reshaped the National Security Council and the Congressional Relations Office, both of which have since become important presidential institutions.

In addition, Kennedy instituted an administrative strategy of the utmost importance in the history of presidential management—using his White House staff as an instrument to control the bureaucracy. He regarded the bureaucracy as an obstacle to changes in domestic and foreign policy.[33] He did not view the bureaucracy as ideologically opposed to his programs, as Nixon later maintained, but instead felt that the logic of the bureaucracy was to resist change. Kennedy's goal was to control and direct the efforts of the bureaucracy—a necessity if he were to achieve his goal of changing the direction of domestic and foreign policy. All of the senior White House aides were caught up in this unheralded struggle: McGeorge Bundy by wielding unprecedented power over the departments and agencies engaged in foreign policy; Theodore Sorenson and his staff by overseeing the domestic side of the government; Larry O'Brien by making sure that the cabinet departments did not put their own interests ahead of the president's interests; Pierre Salinger by doing the same for publicity; and Kenneth O'Donnell, Arthur Schlesinger,

Jr., and Richard Goodwin by acting as presidential troubleshooters throughout the bureaucracy.[34]

Although Lyndon Johnson's administration was concerned with many of the same problems as the Kennedy administration, Johnson's attitude toward the bureaucracy was much more conciliatory. He increased the number of top appointments given to career civil servants and often went out of his way to meet with career officials and to give them a sense of participation in the administration. Johnson was able to offer the carrot to the bureaucracy because Kennedy had already used the stick.[35] However, Johnson was also capable of employing the stick when necessary. He used his White House staff to watch over the affairs of the bureaucracy. Joseph Califano directed a five-man staff that was similar to the Bundy operation in the Kennedy administration; however, his staff was directed at domestic rather than foreign politics and ended as a White House task force authorized to oversee domestic agencies. Johnson's assistants were operatives rather than advisors. They had the authority to oversee, coordinate, and reorganize the federal departments and agencies.

During Richard Nixon's administration, White House staff oversight of the bureaucracy was used as a tool of presidential management. It was a deliberate attempt to use the staff as a counterbureaucracy by placing White House aides in key domestic positions. John Ehrlichman became the head of the domestic council, and many staff members became line officers, developing a chain of command that bypassed the department heads. It became clear that many of the political executives as well as career civil servants were excluded from the decision-making process, and that the subsequent implementation of decisions was closely monitored by the junior White House aides assigned to domestic agencies. Nixon also used the Special Advisor to the President position to bypass the regular department heads. This was the case with Henry Kissinger who, as national security advisor, was more influential in the conduct of foreign affairs than the secretary of state. Nixon attempted to avoid criticism through "doublehatting"—combining the position of White House aide with a departmental secretariat. Kissinger became the national security advisor and the secretary of state as well; other aides became administrators of domestic areas. Each doublehatter had a council or other staff resources, enabling him to promote programs from a perspective broader than his own department's.

Nixon modified his White House staff system at the start of his second term by creating five senior assistant positions: domestic affairs (John Ehrlichman), chief of staff (Bob Haldeman), executive management (Roy Ash), national security (Henry Kissinger), and economic affairs (George Schultz).[36] In effect, three members of the White House staff, the director of the Office of Management and Budget, the National Security Advisor, and the Economic Advisor were responsible for policy decisions during the second Nixon administration. The department secretaries were excluded from the process. The senior assistant structure crumbled in May 1973 with Ehrlichman and Haldeman's resignations under pressure from the Watergate scandal. Until that time, Nixon's use of presidential staff as a counterbureaucracy was so pervasive as to almost bypass the traditional departments and departmental decision-making apparatus. Thus, as presidents increased control over decisions and policy implementation, presidential staffs changed from being the eyes and the ears of the president to a counterbureaucracy in the service of the president.

Another development in personnel manipulation by presidents involves the career civil service. Traditionally, civil service regulations restricted presidents from making changes in career civil service personnel.[37] Presidents can transfer them, reassign them, or even demote them, subject to civil service regulations. Presidents may remove noncareer civil servants and reassign careerists in schedule C positions. However, they have only the most limited powers of removal when dealing with regulatory agencies or commissions or public corporations, and they cannot remove the members of these bodies for policy disagreements with their administrations.

All presidents have attempted to manipulate the career civil service by operating in the "gray" areas of civil service regulations. They have attempted this manipulation so that sympathetic officials could fill key command positions of programs in which each president has a special interest. One method that has been used is to change position classification from the career to the noncareer service. These altered classifications must be approved by the Civil Service Commission.[38]

Normally, this approach is standard practice and is used by most administrations. However, the Nixon administration developed the approach into a fine art. *The Federal Political Personnel Manual*, by Fred Malek, outlines the ways in which the career civil service could be manipulated by the administration. Each department was to set up a personnel office headed by a special assistant secretary. This assistant would write job descriptions to fit a particular individual known to be sympathetic to the administration. Other individuals would receive transfers to undesirable locations, special assignments requiring travel, or trivial work in order to encourage them to resign. The Nixon administration also proposed to Congress that career executives be given positions at the discretion of the department or agency executive-level employees, but the House rejected this proposal.[39]

BUDGETING

A third form of presidential management deals with management techniques closely tied to the executive budget process.[40] These important techniques are planned program budgeting systems, management by objectives, and zero base budgeting. All were designed to introduce greater rationality and control into the budget process. Control of the executive budget process is essential to presidential control of the executive branch. Loss of control of the executive budget process means that the executive branch remains fragmented and directionless, and policy-making remains decentralized and subject to subgovernment control.

The Constitution neither created the budget process nor provided the president with a role in budgeting. According to Richard M. Pious, the "Founding Fathers intended that a Treasury Department would be established by Congress to manage finances and that it would work closely with the legislature to manage finances much as the superintendent of finance had worked with the Continental Congress."[41] The president might recommend to Congress such measures as he thought expedient, and he might propose a financial program, but there was no explicit grant of budgetary authority in Article II. The taxing and spending power mentioned in the Constitution are assigned to Congress in Article I.[42]

Presidents have often attempted to gain control of the executive budget process. By controlling spending levels, the president can impose a chain of command in the executive branch, reward bureaus that carry out his programs, and punish those that do not. However, presidents have rarely been able to control the budget process. Since 1785, when Hamilton (who sought to centralize budgeting power in the Treasury Department) left government, departmental secretaries transmitted their spending estimates directly to Congress, bypassing the Treasury Department and the president. It was not until the Budget and Accounting Act of 1921 that budgetary authority was centralized. This act provided the president and the Bureau of the Budget (BOB) with the authority to compile departmental estimates, revise them, and submit an executive budget to Congress. In the nineteenth century, the president generally stood aside when departmental budgets were compiled, but the Act of 1921 and the procedures used by the BOB made the president a central figure in the executive budget process.[43]

However, the budget process works to subvert presidential control. In the traditional incremental model of budgeting, the program managers and bureau chiefs consider their current expenditures to be their "base," that is, the amount needed to spend in the future to maintain the orgnization's existing activities.[44] The base, including a yearly inflation rate adjustment, becomes untouchable under most conditions. Program managers and bureau chiefs hope to protect "fair shares"—the fair proportion of increments that may come to the department in good times or of decreases the department may be forced to endure during bad times. Budgeting incrementally, officials expect to replicate existing spending within a range of 10 percent in order to continue the bureau's existing programs. This limits the changes the president can make in existing programs through budgeting.[45]

The Johnson administration attempted to change the incremental budgeting process through the planned program budgeting system (PPBS). Early in Johnson's administration, the executive branch experienced a basic shift in program goals. The change aggravated and exposed the organizational deficiencies rooted in the bureaucratic/congressional/interest group axis that dominated the pluralistic process of governmental budget-making and policy-making.[46] PPBS was developed to deal with these deficiencies. According to Allen Schick, evidence suggests that Johnson viewed PPBS as the opening salvo in a major overhaul of the executive branch.[47] PPBS was visualized as a marriage between program planning and budgeting, which would allow for more rationality in the budget process in terms of evaluating social goals and choosing methods to meet these goals.

Although PPBS was familiar to academics, budget officers of private corporations, and some budgetary officials, it was employed in the federal government for the first time during the Johnson administration, in the Department of Defense under Secretary Robert McNamara. The results were so promising that in August 1965, Johnson called a breakfast meeting to inform his cabinet that he was ordering PPBS installed throughout the rest of the executive branch. Unfortunately, PPBS did not live up to expectations. Within six years, the program that was supposed to revolutionize the federal budget-making process was discontinued. The more important reasons for the program's lack of success were:

1. Agencies' planners and budgeteers were overwhelmed by the paperwork required by the program.

2. The introduction of PPBS in the domestic agencies was too abrupt. PPBS was transferred wholesale from the Department of Defense, where it is possible to measure the destructiveness of a new bomb, to the domestic agencies, where it is nearly impossible to measure the benefits of social programs.

3. The program failed to become part of the budget cycle. Faced with an imposed system which they neither designed nor understood, many of the departments reacted by divorcing PPBS from budgeting.[48]

PPBS should not be written off as a total failure, however, because some of the program's concepts and ideas have continued to be employed throughout the bureaucracy.

The Nixon administration introduced a second management technique: management by objectives (MBO). MBO required agency directors to clarify the agency's mission, define specific objectives within the framework of the agency mission, prepare an annual operating plan for each objective, and develop performance reports that measure how well program managers meet the objectives.

A complete MBO program adds two additional steps to this process. The first step results in a genuine redefinition of government priorities. After the agency director's report, the top policymakers (usually political executives and/or legislators) use the director's report and the mission statements drawn from it to establish new initiatives, abolish outdated programs, and redefine agency programs and objectives. This process is not normally shared with career bureaucrats, who tend to define their own programs as crucial. Once the new priorities are announced, the bureaucrats and political executives make strategic program decisions: determining which specializations to stress and how to coordinate them. The political executive may then delegate to the agency directors the responsibility for establishing the specific objectives, operating plans, and measures of performance.

The second step integrates a complete MBO program into other management systems: the budget system, the personnel system, and the information system. These systems are redesigned to support organizational objectives and the operating plans that form their basis. Budget funds are redirected toward the mission; agency personnel who embody the agency's better qualities (as defined by the director) are promoted; and new information is generated to measure the result. Reluctance to integrate MBO into other management programs is the most common source of failure for the program.[49] In such cases, the agency personnel view MBO as a threat; the MBO staff is isolated; budget allocations do not follow objectives; the performance measures become artificial; and the MBO program collapses.

MBO was introduced to give the Executive Office of the President more information about the agency directors' activities, to be used to stimulate directives from presidential appointees ensuring that career officials were responsive and effective in carrying out the work of the administration. MBO was also meant to improve government effectiveness by concentrating attention on results, by giving lower-level managers discretion in adapting their activities to achieve results. The Nixon administration saw MBO not only as a management tool but as a means for grasping the central problem of political direction and government performance.[50]

One of the ironies of MBO is that while it was perceived as a decentralizing system, it provided increased centralization. In theory, members of the agencies were allowed to choose their objectives and the methods to achieve them. However, the information gave the president and his appointees the ability to make political choices about specific agency objectives and methods that they had previously been unable to make because they lacked specific data.

If it were successful, MBO would provide the president with the means to centralize budgeting in the Executive Office and to gain greater control over the executive branch.

In practice, however, the MBO program enjoyed limited success. The objectives submitted to the Office of Management and Budget (OMB) were often of poor quality—too nebulous to be successful or mere carbon copies of presidential wishes. Some agencies and departments more or less ignored the program altogether (the Department of Defense, to cite one example). Moreover, there was a notable failure to integrate the program into other management processes, particularly budgeting. Unlike PPBS, MBO was not a budgeting technique, but it was essential that the objectives be linked to the budget process—something that never occurred.[51]

The Carter administration introduced a third type of management technique directed at the budget process—zero base budgeting (ZBB). ZBB attempts to break the incremental method of budgeting. Agencies previously assumed that they had a protected base and were entitled to incremental increases. ZBB required that each agency start from zero and establish budget needs and justify necessary expenditures by ranking existing and future programs and add-ons according to the agency's objectives. If the program were successful, ZBB would give the president a measure of control over previous uncontrollables in the federal budget.

The ZBB program originated in a bill cosponsored by Senator Edmund Muskie and supported by 50 percent of the Senate in 1976. The Government Economy and Spending Reform Act required a congressional zero base review and evaluation of every government authorization for programs and activities every five years. In addition, it required the director of OMB to develop a program for ZBB in all executive branch departments and agencies.

Past experience would indicate that to be successful, ZBB would have to be supported by the bureaucracy as well as the president and Congress. Unfortunately, this was not the case because of the bureaucracy's legitimate concern that OMB used ZBB not to reorder spending but rather to merely cut budgets. Again, experience suggests that agencies are protective of their budgets and do not respond well to wholesale budget slashes (and perhaps not even to the reordering of spending priorities). Concern was expressed that ZBB resulted in reports that were never read. An additional problem was that ZBB was perceived as an attempt to replace the agencies' existing budget practices. This was almost certainly the case, since the logic of ZBB was to supersede existing incremental budgeting strategies. Conflict of this kind has been shown to be the kiss of death for management techniques in terms of bureaucratic acceptance. Finally, agency personnel have become upset with the rapid replacement of management techniques. Each administration has a pet budget technique that it wants to employ. Given the longevity of the career bureaucracy, many prefer to wait out the administration rather than to give wholehearted acceptance to a particular technique that almost certainly will no longer be employed by a new administration.

Each of the budgeting techniques was developed by an administration to gain greater influence in the budget process, as the president tried to make basic changes in the direction of policy (this was particularly true of Johnson and Nixon). So far, presidents have met with very limited success.[52]

SUMMARY

Presidential management has emerged from presidential frustration over the inability to manage policy implementation. As frustration grew, presidents increasingly turned to management techniques such as reorganization, manipulation of personnel, and budgeting to penetrate the bureaucratic process. The success of presidential management has been hindered by bureaucratic opposition, lack of administrative skill, and perhaps the limitations of the management techniques themselves. Yet because of the lack of alternatives, presidents continue to apply management techniques.

NOTES

1. Because it is impossible to consider all the management attempts since Franklin Roosevelt's administration, this study will focus on the most significant ones.

2. Howard E. McCurdy, in *Public Administration: A Synthesis* (Menlo Park, N.J.: Cummings Publ., 1977), p. 150, defines reorganization as a change in the structure of an organization to improve the effectiveness of the organization, through administrative rationality: an administrative system based on reason rather than on the emotional or political criteria that often influ-

ence administrative decisions. Along the way, the executives also hope to increase their own power.

3. James G. Benze, Jr., "Presidential Reorganization as a Tactical Weapon," *Presidential Studies Quarterly*, vol. 15 (Winter 1986), pp. 145-147.

4. Richard M. Pious, *The American Presidency* (New York: Basic Books, 1979), p. 214.

5. A. J. Wann, *The President as Chief Administrator: A Study of Franklin D. Roosevelt* (Washington, D.C.: Public Affairs Press, 1968), chap. 1. The important features of the act are as follows: The president was allowed to make changes in the executive branch by executive order, while either the House or Congress could veto an executive order by adoption of a resolution of disapproval within sixty days. On March 3, 1933, the act was amended so that the president was permitted to abolish the whole or any part of an executive agency and any of its functions, the sole limitation being that he could not abolish an entire department. The amendment also omitted the congressional veto, so that reorganization could only be defeated by enactment of regular legislation. A second amendment on March 20, 1933, provided that the organizational changes included in an executive order would become effective sixty days after the issuance of that order, whether Congress remained in session or not. The above information is taken from Richard Polenberg, *Reorganizing Roosevelt's Government* (Cambridge: Harvard University Press, 1966), p. 8.

6. Harvey C. Mansfield, "Reorganizing the Federal Executive Branch: The Limits of Institutionalization," *Law and Contemporary Problems*, vol. 35 (1970), p. 462.

7. Harvey C. Mansfield, "Federal Executive Reorganization: Thirty Years Experience," *Public Administration Review*, vol. 29 (1969), pp. 332-344.

8. Otis L. Graham, *Toward a Planned Society* (New York: Oxford University Press, 1976), pp. 58-63.

9. Polenberg, *Reorganizing Roosevelt's Government*, p. 16.

10. Wann, *The President as Chief Administrator*, p. 86.

11. Barry Dean Karl, *Executive Reorganization and Reform in the New Deal* (Cambridge: Harvard University Press, 1963), pp. 226-247.

12. Ibid.

13. Graham, *Toward a Planned Society*, pp. 106-112.

14. Herman Finer, "The Hoover Commission Reports," *Political Science Quarterly*, vol. 64 (1949), p. 405.

15. Graham, *Toward a Planned Society*, pp. 108-109.

16. Ibid., p. 110.

17. Ibid., p. 116.

18. Perhaps in 1952, the Eisenhower administration might have turned the clock back to 1920, but by 1955, the opportunity had passed. The Ei-

senhower administration had given up any notion of attempting to repeal the New Deal, and the Democrats (then in control of Congress) and the bureaucrats would have been likely to defeat such a move.

19. Among the authors who have suggested this possibility, Herman Finer, "The Hoover Commission Reports," *Political Science Quarterly*, vol. 64 (1949), makes the strongest case. However, given the limited success that future presidents have had in attempting to impose their wishes on the bureaucracy, it is unlikely that such a change would have been successful even if Truman had desired it.

20. Others on the council were John Connally, former governor of Texas; George P. Baker, dean of the Harvard Graduate School of Business Administration; Frederick R. Kappel, former chairman of the board of American Telephone and Telegraph Company; Walter N. Thayer, president of Whitney Communications; and Richard M. Paget, president of the consulting firm of Cresap, McCormick, and Paget.

21. Richard P. Nathan, *The Plot That Failed* (New York: John Wiley, 1975), p. 88-93.

22. Peter Woll and Rochelle Jones, "Against One-Man Rule: Bureaucratic Defense in Depth," *The Nation*, vol. 217 (1973), pp. 229-233.

23. As Joel D. Aberbach and Bert A. Rockman suggest in "Clashing Beliefs Within the Executive Branch," *American Political Science Review*, vol. 70 (June 1976), pp. 456-568, a large portion of the bureaucracy was indeed ideologically opposed to the objectives of the Nixon administration. However, they do not demonstrate the impact of the ideological belief system on subsequent behavior.

24. As Randall B. Ripley and Grace A. Franklin demonstrate in *Congress, the Bureaucracy, and Public Policy* (Homewood, Ill.: Dorsey Press, 1976), the different policy areas involved with domestic policy also relate to a president's degree of strength in controlling domestic agencies.

25. Thomas E. Cronin was one of the first presidential scholars to refer to the inner versus outer cabinets and the impact of the department's location on departmental–presidential relations. Cronin's breakdown of the outer cabinet departments is as follows: Agriculture; Interior; Transportation; Health, Education, and Welfare; Housing and Urban Development; Labor; and Commerce. Thomas E. Cronin, *The State of the Presidency* (Boston: Little, Brown, 1975), p. 190.

26. Richard M. Pious, *The American Presidency* (New York: Basic Books, 1979), p. 218.

27. Ibid., p. 243.

28. Ibid., p. 218.

29. Richard Neustadt, "Approaches to Staffing the Presidency: Notes on FDR and JFK," *American Political Science Review*, vol. 57 (1963), p. 856.

30. Patrick Anderson, *The President's Men* (New York: Doubleday, 1968), p. 91.

31. Anderson (pp. 85-95) details the importance of Dr. John Roy Steelman as assistant to the president and Clark Clifford as special counsel to the president, as well as the personal and bureaucratic disputes between them in the Truman administration.

32. Patricia Florestano, "The Characteristics of White House Staff Appointees from Truman to Nixon," *Presidential Studies Quarterly*, vol. 11 (Fall 1979).

33. Anderson, *The President's Men*, p. 134.

34. Ibid., p. 202.

35. Ibid., p. 301-302.

36. Pious, *The American Presidency*, p. 245.

37. Hugh Heclo, in *A Government of Strangers* (Washington, D.C.: Brookings Institution, 1977), pp. 19-34, gives an excellent discussion of how civil service regulations affect presidential management.

38. This, of course, is prior to the Civil Service Reform Act of 1978. Now, changes would be referred to the Office of Personnel and Management.

39. David A. Caputo and Richard L. Cole, in "Presidential Control of the Senior Civil Service: Assessing the Strategies of the Nixon Years," *American Political Science Review*, vol. 73 (June 1979), pp. 399-413, demonstrate just how effective Nixon was in changing the ideological makeup of the civil service.

40. Louis Fischer, in *Presidential Spending Power* (Princeton, N.J.: Princeton University Press, 1975), p. 3, draws the distinction between the allocation and spending aspects of budgeting. As Fischer demonstrates, the president has a great deal more power in the spending phase of budgeting than he has in the allocation phase. Because the administrative techniques discussed in this chapter deal mainly with the allocation phase, that phase will be the main focus of the study. Therefore, from this point on, references to the budget process will concern the allocation rather than spending phase of budgeting.

41. Pious, *The American Presidency*, p. 256.

42. Louis Fischer, in *Presidential Spending Power* (Princeton, N.J.: Princeton University Press, 1975), demonstrates that presidents have developed constitutional arguments to support a variety of spending powers (impoundment, transfers, reprogramming, and so on) that have been used to control the spending phase of budgeting.

43. As shown by Fischer, in *Presidential Spending Power*, p. 10, it is incorrect to suggest that the president was completely divorced from the budget process prior to the Budget and Accounting Act of 1921. Rather,

that act symbolizes a change toward greater centralization of budget authority in the executive.

44. Aaron Wildavsky, *The Politics of the Budgetary Process* (Boston: Little, Brown, 1974), gives the best description of the incremental budget-making process.

45. Moreover, the close links between many of the bureaus and congressional committees that control budget allocations allow the agencies to make "end runs" around the president and the Office of Management and Budget, in order to restore cuts that have been made in the compilation of the federal budget.

46. William Gorham, "PPBS: Its Scope and Limits," *The Public Interest*, vol. 8 (Summer 1967), p. 5.

47. Allen Schick, "Systems, Politics, and Systems Budgeting," *Public Administration Review*, vol. 29 (1969), p. 143.

48. Allen Schick, "A Death in the Bureaucracy: The Demise of Federal PPB," *Public Administration Review*, vol. 29 (1969), pp. 146-155.

49. McCurdy, *Public Administration*, pp. 4-5.

50. Richard Rose, *Managing Presidential Objectives* (New York: Free Press, 1976), pp. 12-30.

51. Jerry McCaffery, "MBO and the Federal Budgeting Process," *Public Administration Review*, vol. 36 (1976), p. 34.

52. It is interesting to note that budgeting techniques proposed by the past three administrations come from the generic approach to public administration, and in several cases directly from the Harvard Business School. For example, PPBS had its origin in the Harvard Business School, and many of the earlier advocates of the program in the Johnson administration (particularly the younger members of the Bureau of the Budget) were graduates of the Harvard Business School. Like PPBS, MBO also had its origins in the business school tradition and was first employed in private industry, not the government. Moreover, those who employed the program had close connections to the Harvard Business School. Fred Malek was a graduate of that institution, as were many members of his staff. Several critics of the MBO program questioned whether Nixon was in fact fashioning an MBO staff consisting of Harvard Business School graduates who were loyal only to the president, and then placing them in the agencies where they would have the primary responsibility for making the program work. All this occurred at the expense of the career budget examiners and helped to heighten the animosity between the career civil service and the Nixon administration. Finally, ZBB also had its roots in academe and industry. Perhaps the lack of success that the budget techniques have achieved points to the greater importance of the "public" in public administration.

4

Management in the Carter Administration

INTRODUCTION

All modern presidents have been interested in increasing their control over policy implementation, but their methods and rates of success have varied. Although there are similarities in the range of administrative techniques from which they have drawn, each modern president has chosen a unique set of techniques. Presidents have also brought to policy administration their own orientation toward management and differing collections of personal and political skills. Together, the administrative techniques and personal and political skills make up, respectively, the external and internal dimensions of presidential power. The manner in which each president employs these dimensions of power creates that president's management style. Moreover, differences in presidents' management styles will be reflected in differences in their ability to control the implementation of policy.

MANAGEMENT STYLE

Many authors have studied a president's management program, but few have brought together the various aspects of presidential management in order to make historical comparisons.[1] The few authors that have attempted a comparative approach have concentrated on presidential decision making.[2]

However, when assessing management styles, management techniques designed to affect policy implementation are as important as decision-making styles that affect policy choice. Also, an assessment of the external dimension of presidential power should deal with more than one variable. For example, an assessment of the external dimension of management style of the Carter administration would include the president's use of staff (both in decision-making and oversight capacities), the manipulation of personnel (political executives and career civil service), reorganization, and involvement in the budget-making process.

There is, however, another dimension to both presidential power and a president's management style. This dimension is the president's orientation toward management and his collection of personal and political skills. As presidential power is a relational concept, it is only natural that the president's personal and political skills, especially those skills necessary for interacting with other elites, would form an important dimension of power, and thus management style.

Ross Clayton and William Lammers have shown that top federal officials have a general concept of the components of presidential skills that are effective vis-à-vis other political elites.[3] One of the more important political skills is the president's ability to sense the political realities of the social context and the expectations of other political actors.

The personal skills involve the president's character—especially his level of self-confidence, intelligence, vision, flexibility, and courage. The president's electoral skills include, for example, his ability to maintain electoral confidence while "manipulating" the public into a position congruent with his administration on important policy issues.

Although these skills are considered to be an important component of the internal dimension of power, it is obvious that different presidents will have these skills in different degrees and will employ them in different ways. These differences also represent differences in management styles.

PRESIDENTIAL POWER AND MANAGEMENT IN THE CARTER ADMINISTRATION

To analyze the Carter management style, it is necessary to understand the relation of power and management in the Carter administration. Briefly stated, the Carter administration used management techniques in an effort to increase presidential power precisely because of Carter's inability to exercise traditional sources of presidential influence and authority to control policy implementation. Moreover, as the administration progressed, greater emphasis was placed on management techniques as presidential influence in policy implementation declined.

Presidential power rests in part on institutional and personal authority, and for a variety of reasons, both were in short supply in the Carter administration. In the ten years preceding the Carter administration, there was a reduction in the president's institutional authority. His constitutional authority was curbed in a number of important areas, including war-making and impoundment. Moreover, Vietnam, Watergate, and the president's inability to deal with serious economic and social problems combined to undermine the influence and authority that the presidential office has commanded. The evidence of the decline of presidential credibility on which institutional authority is partially based was substantial and ranged from public opinion polls to the impressions of small children and the essays of political commentators.[4] After Watergate, it became fashionable to be critical of the "imperial presidency" and, in fact, a school of presidential revisionism emerged.[5] As a result, it may be argued that the Carter administration did not have the same level of traditional influence as other presidents.

Carter also did not have the personal authority (or prestige and credibility) to overcome this lack of institutional authority. Although even his critics admit that Carter was one of the more honest presidents, there were so many questions raised about his leadership abilities that it became a main issue in the 1980 presidential primaries. Public opinion polls throughout Carter's first term demonstrated that he did not have overwhelming support in his own party or in the general electorate.[6] Several observers suggested that Carter also lacked the network of Washington connections that often serve as a source of information as well as influence for a president.[7] It is clear that Carter's role as "political outsider," while effective in his election campaign, hindered him as president.

Therefore, while traditional sources of presidential power, influence, and authority have not generally proven effective in providing presidents with control over the implementation process, Carter found even those sources weakened through recent political developments and his own actions. As a result, he relied heavily on management techniques to increase presidential power and to gain control over policy implementation.

THE CARTER MANAGEMENT STYLE: THE INTERNAL DIMENSION

It is necessary to analyze the collection of personal skills, attitudes, and perceptions, or the internal dimension of power, that Carter brought to the process of governing. James Fallows argues that President Carter's personal and political skills were lacking in three important areas: sophistication, ability to explain goals, and passion.[8] Indeed, several authors have suggested that Carter, in essence, has a "managerial mind."[9] This is represented in the way in which Carter organizes information and approaches his work. According to Nicholas Lemman, Carter is above all else a perfectionist and is almost physically unable to be cursory when personally involved. Carter is a man who wants everything to be right the first time, not the second. He is also fanatically devoted to self-improvement, to the point of memorizing the classical music that is played while he works and of turning a vacation at Gettysburg into a seminar on Civil War history. Ultimately, Carter is an organized man who would have liked to have been remembered as a topflight manager of government.

This orientation toward management caused James L. Sundquist to identify the administration of politics as a major theme in Carter's administration.[10] The "administration of politics" refers to the Carter administrative and decision-making styles, which resulted in the political aspects of governing being eliminated and replaced with management. This tendency toward the administration of politics is represented in several aspects of the Carter administration. First is Carter's "attention to detail and procedure rather than politics," and his preference for making quantitative rather than qualitative judgments.[11] That tendency is further illustrated in the way Carter used his staff to carry out policy rather than to advise.

The desire to avoid politics in the governing process extends to the way Carter used people (or perhaps in the way Carter did not use people). As president, Carter was remarkably inept at utilizing the people who could be helpful to his administration. This tendency stands in complete contrast to the image of Carter as "campaigner." For Carter, using people was a political act and proper while campaigning but should be separated from the act of governing, which is "managerial."

In avoiding politics, Carter was in direct contrast to other presidents, especially Lyndon Johnson. Whereas Carter was fascinated by the administrative, Johnson reveled in the rough and tumble of political intrigue. Carter was ineffective in using people who could be helpful; Johnson was an expert at using people (critics might argue that he did so for nefarious reasons), and aides speak of the "Johnson treatment." Carter often seemed reticent and withdrawn, while Johnson was gregarious and outgoing. Given these differences, it is small wonder they had different attitudes toward governing.

This brief overview suggests that President Carter may have been weak in the internal dimension of power. His basic orientation toward management was to stress the techniques (external dimension of power) rather than the skills (internal dimension of power) of management. This appears to be at least partially the result of Carter's natural inclination toward the orderliness of administrative techniques, but it also stems from his lack of political skill. The net result in the Carter presidency was a heavy reliance on the external dimension of power.

THE CARTER MANAGEMENT STYLE: THE EXTERNAL DIMENSION

From the beginning of his campaign for the presidency to the end of his first administration, Carter made clear his commitment to management techniques to increase presidential control over the bureaucracy. In an interview with Bill Moyers in 1978, Carter remarked:

I saw quite early in my administration as governor of Georgia that we had an undeserved reputation as Democrats of not being fiscally responsible and not being competent in management. One of the major thrusts of my governorship was to reorganize the government, to get control of the bureaucracy, and to cut taxes, to budget carefully, and I ran my campaign for President on that platform.[12]

In an earlier news conference, Carter indicated that he realized the first step in management was to gain control over the federal bureaucracy, and that such a step would not be easy.

Before I became President, I realized and was warned that dealing with the bureaucracy would be one of the worst problems I would ever have to face. It has been even worse than I had anticipated. Of all the steps that we can take to make government more efficient and effective, reforming the civil service is the most important of all.[13]

Such problems demanded the creation of a management program.

PERSONNEL

Carter initiatives in personnel management were mainly in the areas of staffing and civil service reform. Carter entered the White House publicly committed to an administrative structure that would avoid the excesses of the Nixon presidency. Indeed, Carter's approach to staffing reflected the Nixon administration's negative influence. There would be no chief of staff under Carter. Instead, the president would be accessible to all members of his administration, while cabinet officials would be in charge of their own departments—not the president's White House staff.[14] Carter announced that he would institute "cabinet government," with cabinet officials maintaining the primary responsibility for activities in their departments. The presidential staff would be loosely organized and work cooperatively with cabinet officials in designing and implementing policy.[15]

Subsequent changes in the White House staff/cabinet relations suggest that Carter became disenchanted with cabinet government. The decentralization of power in the cabinet and the White House staff offices, when combined with the centralization of the final decision-making authority in the Oval Office, left the administration with a multitude of semi-autonomous fiefdoms, quarreling bitterly among themselves and speaking with different voices to the public.[16] The president and his closest advisors, along with Carter's critics, recognized that cabinet government led not only to poor coordination, poor implementation, and bickering among cabinet and staff members over policy questions but also, from the White House perspective, to disloyalty to the administration on the part of several key cabinet officials.

Consequently, in the summer of 1979, Carter moved to centralize power in the executive office through personnel changes. Secretary of Health, Education, and Welfare Joseph Califano and Treasury Secretary W. Michael Blumenthal were fired, and the following day, Hamilton Jordan was named White House chief of staff. Other changes included firing Transportation Secretary Brock Adams, accepting the resignation of Energy Secretary James Schlesinger, and moving Patricia Harris from Housing and Urban Development to Health, Education, and Welfare (HEW). Subsequent to the cabinet shake-up, Jordan ordered cabinet secretaries to fill out "report cards" on their top subordinates, grading them for their ability as well as their loyalty. In addition, the White House replaced fifty or sixty subcabinet officials with White House–approved appointees (six or seven new appointments at the Department of Energy; four each at Defense, Justice, and HEW; and four at the Office of Management and Budget).[17]

Carter also made changes in the presidential staff. In redesigning the staff structure, he sought to draw a clearer line of command without threatening the senior staff. Hamilton Jordan emerged as the most influential as the chief of staff and described his role in the following manner:

I'm going to run the White House. I'm not bashful or apologetic about it. He [Carter] doesn't want me nor will I try to mold the senior staff into a cohesive unit and resolve disputes and conflicts here at the White House and I will try to foster better relations between the White House and the Cabinet. I don't think that it is incompatible with my responsibilities. I don't expect to impede access to the Cabinet; that dimension of my responsibility has been exaggerated.[18]

Even though Jordan viewed his new capacity as helping to resolve problems, he obviously exerted enormous influence on the

decision-making process since he controlled the selection of participants, the timing, the political strategy, and the eventual presenta-
tion of problems to the president. It became apparent that controlling the administrative apparatus was also part of Jordan's new
responsibilities.

Several parallels can be drawn between the White House
staff/cabinet relations in the Nixon and Carter administrations. At
first, the Nixon administration allowed cabinet officers considerable
independence in running their departments but later sought to reduce their authority and to exert control over the departments by
establishing a counterbureaucracy in the White House.[19] Policy-
making was centralized in the White House, and Nixon's expanded
staff had the authority to clear agency appointments. Loyalists from
the White House office were transplanted to the cabinet departments, and the senior White House staff operations became more
political.

Many of these same changes occurred in the Carter administration, indicating that this administration conformed to a historical
pattern. As the distance between the White House and the executive
departments increases, presidents become frustrated with lack of
bureaucratic support. When presidents observe cabinet secretaries
becoming more closely identified with their special clientele, they
look inward for support.

Another historical pattern emerged in Carter's use of personnel.
Presidents rarely pay systematic attention to the most obvious, direct, and effective method for achieving managerial competence:
filling key managerial positions in the executive branch with professional managers capable of administering large organizations. Instead, the prevailing attitude, as noted by Alan Dean, seems to be
"neo-Jacksonianism," the notion that any citizen can do any public
job.[20] Top administrative posts are usually reserved as rewards for
political loyalists.

This practice was even more pronounced in the Carter administration because Carter's inner circle was made up of political loyalists from Georgia who were unfamiliar with the Washington scene.
Therefore, the administration was unable to identify and select people with proven track records as public managers, and Carter ended
up with senior staff and advisors who compounded rather than

compensated for his personal weaknesses. Carter's appointment of Bert Lance to the Office of Management and Budget (OMB) was a perfect example of cronyism winning out over management. Nor did Carter compensate for Lance's shortcomings by searching for experienced managers to staff the remaining positions. Of the ten political appointees in OMB, only one had worked in the executive branch of the federal government.[21] Several Carter cabinet officials had no reputation as managers and failed to ensure that their political appointees were chosen for their management expertise. Because cabinet officials chose their associates, they reduced the number of outright incompetents with which cabinet members are usually saddled for patronage reasons, but they also made spotty management choices. In staffing the remaining political posts in the department hierarchies (undersecretaries, their deputies, and the heads of agencies and bureaus), most department heads were preoccupied with the capacity to make policy, not to administer it.

The reasons why modern presidents are reluctant to appoint proven public managers to high-level posts in the executive branch must be examined. The Carter experience indicates that proven public managers (for example, Califano, Blumenthal, and Schlesinger) are often the first to be removed from an administration because they go into business for themselves. Presidents are looking for political executives who will represent the president's interests and objectives, not their own. However, time and patronage considerations usually preclude even finding appointees loyal to the president.

The Carter administration was also interested in civil service reform to gain greater control over the career civil service personnel.[22] The Carter Civil Service Reform program, signed into law on October 13, 1978, had the following main features:

1. *New Agencies*—This program created the Office of Personnel Management, which took over personnel management functions, and the Merit Systems Protection Board, which is a new board of appeals for employees' grievances.

2. *Merit System*—Merit system principles and prohibited personnel practices were defined. The bill also spelled out procedures for investigating and punishing prohibited personnel practices, including reprisals against employees who blow the whistle on government wrongdoing.

3. *Incompetent Workers*—Managers were given slightly more authority in firing incompetent workers, although not as much as Carter had originally proposed.

4. *New Senior Service Corps*—A new Senior Executive Service (SES) was authorized, consisting of eight thousand top federal managers and policymakers (Congress exempted several intelligence agencies from SES). Employees of SES would be eligible for cash bonuses and less tenure and would be more easily transferred between departments and agencies.

5. *Merit Pay*—Merit pay was established for GS 13 through GS 15 Civil Service positions, and most raises would be based on detailed evaluations of individual performances.

6. *Federal Labor Practices*—This program created the Federal Labor Relations Authority, which is comparable to the National Labor Relations Board for private sector employees and was established to hear complaints about unfair labor practices in federal employment.

7. *Employee Limit*—A ceiling was placed on the total number of federal employees established for fiscal years 1979-1981.

8. *Unions*—The rights of federal employees to join labor unions and bargain collectively on certain personnel practices and policies was established in law. Previously, these rights were granted only by executive order subject to change by the president with Congressional review.[23]

The only major Carter proposal rejected by Congress was the curtailment of veterans preference in federal hiring.

Most modern presidents have tried to extend their control over the career civil service through the selective use of hirings and transfers. Generally, they were unable to accomplish more in this area because of the special civil service codes that protect the rights of career civil servants from political pressures. Therefore, the Carter administration's immediate aim was to reform the civil service itself, a move that had long been advocated by political scientists as well as public administrators. In 1978, Carter touched on the importance of civil service reform to his administration:

Two months ago, I submitted to the Congress a comprehensive program of reform for the civil service. My aim has been to clear a path for honest, hardworking, and industrious civil servants and to give them the tools to get the job done. I want to reward competence and punish the unresponsive who cheat the American taxpayer and give all governments a bad name.

And I want to make government more effective by establishing clear assignments of responsibility and authority. We need to put merit back in the
merit system. We are trying to do that in a way that honors and protects
every Federal employee's rights while giving managers in the Federal government the authority to do their job. It is virtually impossible now to
discipline those Federal employees who fail to perform. This is an issue of
efficiency and good management, but it goes beyond that.[24]

Later, Carter remarked:

This is a crucial element of my attempt to control the bureaucracy in the
Federal government, and it is such a burning issue in the minds of the
American people to finally do something about waste and to control the
Federal bureaucracy that I am really convinced that the House members of
Congress will not go home and face the electorate not having acted upon
it.[25]

However, were the Carter civil service reforms intended to improve efficiency or to punish the bureaucracy and gain control
through intimidation? Take, for example, the central part of the program: the Senior Executive Service (SES). The SES involved the creation of a pool of some eight thousand managers above the level
of GS 15 who are held accountable for the success of the programs
they administer. These administrators are evaluated through the SES
evaluation system, featuring assessments of managerial performance and incentive pay awards for those who are deemed "worthy." Those not deemed worthy are removed from the service and
returned to the larger career civil service. It was hoped that the SES
program would be successful in creating a pool of accomplished
and professional administrators that could be drawn upon to fill
managerial positions and to redress the problem caused by the politicalization of the civil service.

There is evidence to suggest that these characteristics of the SES
system affected the degree of support career civil servants were
willing to give the SES. Naomi B. Lynn and Richard Evaden argue
that there was little support among top-level executives in the federal bureaucracy, and that bureaucrats were not convinced that the
proposed changes would bring about the desired efficiency and
effectiveness.[26] Others suggested that career executives were reluctant to enter the SES program, and that those who did enter did so
out of fear that their careers would be held back if they did not.

The Carter administration put more emphasis on the manipulation of personnel than has any other modern president except Nixon. Carter's orientation was very different, however. Initially, little emphasis was placed on political appointees' importance for management, although later developments indicate that the Carter administration's interest in political appointees grew.

Nearly the same conclusion can be drawn from Carter's use of staff as a management tool. Early in the Carter administration, there was a noticeable effort to avoid using staff in an oversight capacity. However, the July 1979 shuffling of the president's staff and the cabinet firings indicated a larger role for the staff in decision making and management, and a more tightly controlled role for cabinet officers.

The use of reform to gain control over the civil service represented a genuine innovation in the application of administrative techniques to presidential management. At best, the Carter administration's reforms represented the development of an institutional capacity for personnel management. At worst, they may also have represented reform through intimidation. In either case, the reforms served to increase presidential power and the president's management capacity.

REORGANIZATION

Presidents have also attempted to use reorganization to gain control over the executive departments and agencies. Reorganization efforts highlight not only the institutional struggle for power in the sharp conflict between the president and the various bureaucracies but also the limits of presidential power. For agencies, reorganization involves the gain or loss of autonomy, prestige, and funds. With or without the acquiescence of its chief, a threatened bureaucracy will muster the support of its clientele when threatened by reorganization.[27]

The Carter administration's first reorganization effort involved the Executive Office of the President. Throughout his presidential campaign, Carter promised to reduce the payroll of the Executive Office and to cut the White House staff by one-third. The reorganization plan submitted to Congress was designed to accomplish the following:

1. Reduce the number of full-time staff positions in the Executive Office of the President from 1,712 to 459, providing a net savings of six million dollars.

2. Cut the number of Executive Office units from 19 to 12.

3. Trim the size of the White House staff from 485 to 351 (28 percent).

4. Establish a new policy management system designed to ensure that the Executive Office of the President brings the full resources of the government to bear on presidential decisions and serves the president by developing policy agendas and assigning responsibility.

5. Consolidate the administrative functions of each segment of the Executive Office of the President into a new central administrative unit.[28]

This reorganization effort contained a mixture of the symbolic and management purposes of reorganization (or as Dom Bonafede suggested, the mixture of smoke and substance).[29] On the surface, the Carter reorganization plan fulfilled many of the Carter campaign promises—particularly, fewer personnel and less expenditures. However, the absolute numbers of personnel and expenditures were not decreased as much as the administration proclaimed publicly. The actual number of personnel was reduced by transferring Executive Office employees to other parts of the executive branch, where they were still on call to serve the president. In fact, staffing developments pushed the absolute number of Executive Office personnel to new highs. Regardless of the absolute numbers involved, it was not clear that the elimination of personnel and expenditures by itself would lead to improved management. It did, however, allow Carter to give the appearance of action and gain a reputation as a competent manager without really engaging in the power politics of reorganization.[30]

The reorganization plan also sought to reorganize the institutional structure for developing and coordinating policy in the Executive Office by replacing the Domestic Council with the Domestic Policy Staff.[31] The Domestic Policy Staff, under the leadership of Stuart Eizenstat, became an effective force for the coordination and development of domestic policy. In this respect, the reorganization fulfilled specific management needs.

Major reorganizations in the executive branch often test the limits of presidential power, as agencies successfully resist presidential intrusions on their turf and weaken presidential management efforts. Several of the Carter reorganization efforts demonstrate these limits.[32]

In 1978, Carter's Reorganization Project drew up four neatly integrated and comprehensive plans to consolidate fragmented programs in four policy areas (economic and community development, natural resources, food and nutrition, and trade) into four cabinet departments: Development Assistance; Natural Resources; Food and Nutrition; and Trade, Technology, and Industry. One plan would have taken the economic development programs from Commerce and Agriculture and transferred them to Housing and Urban Development (HUD), which would then have been renamed the Department of Developmental Assistance. The Interior Department would have become the Department of Natural Resources and received additional programs dealing with natural resources from Commerce, Agriculture, and other agencies. The Departments of Commerce and Agriculture would have received compensation for the programs they lost. Agriculture would have become the Department of Food and Nutrition and would have been given a newly defined departmental mission, although no new programs. Commerce would have gained programs related to international trade from the State and Treasury Departments and been retitled the Department of Trade, Technology, and Industry. Because the plans neither created nor destroyed executive departments, it was felt that the proposals could be sent to Congress as reorganization plans not requiring additional legislation. It was hoped that if the plans did not create passionate enemies, then they would not have to create passionate friends.

It was soon discovered that the plans did, in fact, create passionate enemies by causing friction within the cabinet. HUD Secretary Patricia Harris (who stood to gain the most from the proposed reorganization) actively campaigned for the plans, while Commerce Secretary Juanita Kreps (who stood to lose) opposed the reorganization. Agricultural Secretary Robert Bergland opposed the plans, having the luxury of impassioned rural interests lobbying against the plans. The congressional committees overseeing the program schedules to be shifted between departments also supported the status quo.[33] The most vehement objections to the reorganization came from the interest group elites whose cozy relations with the affected agencies were threatened. Several Washington observers suggested that the interest groups were motivated more by their own parochial interests than by the inconsistencies associated with the reorganization.[34] For example, rural groups feared the loss of their clout in the Agriculture Department if rural development programs were turned over to the Department of Development Assistance. Specifically, they objected to the transfer of Farmer Home Administration programs because they feared that the new department would subordinate rural interests to big-city programs.

On the advice of his personal staff, in response to pressures by the triple alliances, Carter revised the reorganization plans. The Natural Resources reorganization remained essentially the same, while the economic development programs were separated from community development programs and sent to Congress as part of the Economic Development Assistance Renewal Act. The other reorganization plans were dropped. Even with this modified plan, Carter received pressure from agricultural interests, forcing him to drop the plan to create a Department of Natural Resources.[35] Carter thereby became the sixth president to attempt to reorganize natural resource programs and to fail.

Carter had more success with his second reorganization, even though it exhibited the same pattern of conflict. The reorganization was designed to create a Department of Education. As originally suggested by the President's Reorganization Project, the Department of Education was to be very narrowly focused, consisting exclusively of HEW's Office of Education.[36] Carter's advisors thought that a narrowly focused plan would avoid the opposition created by a broader plan, and that once the department was established, additional programs could be transferred to it. This "political" approach was rejected by Carter, who wanted a more inclusive plan, consolidating all education programs into one department. However, even this limited reorganization proposal gained the animosity of HEW Secretary Joseph Califano, who subsequently opposed the plan. As the reorganization plan expanded, the ranks of the opposition swelled to include the Defense Department, the Agriculture Department, and the Bureau of Indian Affairs, as well as the interest groups and congressional committees associated with the programs. Although not successful in completely thwarting the creation of the Department of Education, the triple alliances managed to remove many of their "pet" programs from the reorganization plan.

The third Carter reorganization was the creation of the Energy Department. Although the Energy reorganization sought to centralize many of the existing energy programs into a single department, there was comparatively little opposition to the reorganization. One reason for the lack of opposition was the relative newness of the energy programs. Many of the programs were so new that strong triple alliances had yet to form around the programs. For example, the main elements of the Energy Department consisted of the two-year-old Energy Research and Development Administration and the three-year-old Federal Energy Administration. Both agencies were transferred to the new department, where their functions were to be scrambled and rearranged to develop better coordination of and control over energy programs.[37]

During his first term, Carter made a strong effort to achieve greater control over domestic programs through reorganization. He was successful in consolidating the major energy programs; he also had success in the area of education. However, Carter was unable to reorganize domestic programs in other areas.

BUDGETING

The final area of presidential management is budgeting. Previously, presidents had only marginally been involved in the budget process. However, in the last decade, presidents have increasingly faced the realization that control of policy implementation must be preceded by control of the budget process. Therefore, presidents have sought budgeting techniques to break up the triple alliances of the incremental model of budgeting in order to gain greater control over the executive budget. Unless the president can somehow gain control of the budget process, many of the programs in the executive branch will remain outside presidential influence.[38] Johnson had planned program budgeting systems; Nixon had management by objectives; and Carter had zero base budgeting (ZBB).

Carter's interest in ZBB evolved during his first term as governor of Georgia, when he became the first to institute a ZBB program on a government-wide basis. ZBB was designed to give the president greater control over the budget by forcing agencies to:

1. Analyze what would happen if they reduced all of their programs to the absolute minimum of funding.
2. Examine the benefits that would result from beefing up each program.
3. Rank all of their basic programs and add-ons from most to least valuable.[39]

In theory, ZBB would require agencies to review heretofore unexamined parts of the budget, hopefully providing the president with more access to the budget process. However, the early returns on ZBB did not suggest much success for the president.

Evaluating the first Carter budget, Allen Schick suggested that "the first president to promise a zero base budget has delivered the most incremental financial statement since Wildavsky canonized that form of budget making more than a dozen years ago."[40] Schick argues that when inflation is added to the equation, there was almost no exercise of presidential power. Virtually every function, subfunction, and major program was funded at or slightly higher than its prior service level.[41] Subsequent evaluations of Carter budgets also indicate little change brought about by the use of ZBB.[42]

However, the new budget system was not entirely without success. The new budget system was more speedily installed throughout the bureaucracy than previously expected, indicating at least a degree of bureaucratic acceptance. In addition, ZBB was much more than an ancillary submission, merely supplementing the standard budget documents that continued to receive the lion's share of attention. The core budget estimates submitted by most federal agencies conformed to ZBB guidelines.[43] Unlike planned program budgeting systems and management by objectives, ZBB was not divorced from the basic process of preparing agency budgets. By using ZBB, agencies were better able to coordinate programs and to involve line managers in budget decisions. Moreover, ZBB's ability to force agencies to establish program priorities and to generate quantitative data assessments of the consequences of various funding levels is considered of prime importance for presidential management.

All this aside, however, it is not clear that ZBB has been a means for increasing presidential power. In this respect, Carter's use of ZBB fits the pattern of recent presidential budgeting initiatives: Limited success has been the rule rather than the exception. Although

ZBB may hold greater hope for the future than previous techniques, budgeting continued to resist presidential management through the end of the Carter administration.

SUMMARY

The Carter administration was greatly interested in using administrative techniques to gain greater control over policy implementation. However, in each of the areas considered, Carter met with mixed success in converting administrative techniques into presidential power. Carter consistently failed to "sell" his management initiatives to the bureaucracy and Congress, particularly in the areas of reorganization and budgeting. The president failed to use his personal and political skills to convince those affected by the administrative techniques to either cooperate or to submit and accept. Therefore, while Carter made a strong effort in the external dimension of political power with regard to management (the use of administrative techniques), the internal dimension was not used as successfully.

NOTES

1. Generally, authors concerned with management focus their efforts on a single administration, such as Richard P. Nathan, *The Plot That Failed* (New York: John Wiley and Sons, 1975), which deals primarily with the Nixon administration, or a single management technique, such as staffing across several administrations, as in Patrick Anderson, *The President's Men* (New York: Doubleday, 1968).

2. For example, Michael Gregory Fullington, "Presidential Management and Executive Scandal," *Presidential Studies Quarterly*, vol. 10 (Winter 1979), p. 192.

3. Ross Clayton and William Lammers, "Presidential Leadership Reconsidered: Contemporary View of Top Federal Officials," *Presidential Studies Quarterly*, vol. 8 (Winter 1978), pp. 237-244. Clayton and Lammers base the skill dimension on Neustadt's view of "presidential power," the character dimension on James David Barber's assessment of "presidential character," and the electoral dimension on Erwin Hargrove's assessment of "electoral trust."

4. For example, Howard Tolley, *Children and War: Socialization to International Conflict* (New York: Teachers College Press, 1973), found

that the conflicts of the late 1960s and early 1970s changed the way small children viewed the president. Also, F. Christopher Arterton, "The Impact of Watergate on Children's Attitudes Toward Political Authority," *Political Science Quarterly*, vol. 89 (1974), p. 272, found similar changes in attitude related to Watergate.

5. Some refer to this tradition as the "black hat" view of the presidency; see Myron Q. Hale, "Presidential Influence, Authority, and Power and Economic Policy," in *Toward a Humanistic Science of Politics: Essays in Honor of Francis Dunham Woarmuth*, ed. Dalmas H. Nelson and Richard L. Sklar (New York: University Press of America, 1983). Works in this tradition range from the psychoanalytic approach of James David Barber, *Presidential Character* (Englewood Cliffs, N.J.: Prentice-Hall, 1976) to the class analysis of Bruce Miroff, *Pragmatic Illusions* (New York: David McKay Co., 1976) to the combined psychoanalytic and class analysis of Victor E. Wolfenstein, "The Two Wars of Lyndon Johnson," *Politics and Society*, vol. 3 (December 1974). More recent literature suggests that this tradition may be waning, with advocates for presidential power in resurgence.

6. Like most presidents, Carter had his ups and downs in the public opinion polls. In 1979, for example, Carter went from an Egyptian–Israeli peace treaty signing (March), where his ratings hit their peak for the year, to the summer gasoline shortage and the lowest public approval of his presidency (July, approval 28 percent), and then came back at year's end as a result of internal changes in the executive branch and his response to the Iranian hostage situation. However, later polls showed him losing some of the support he gained in late 1979 and early 1980. Larry Light, "Carter's Year," *Congressional Quarterly* (January 5, 1980), pp. 43-45.

7. James Fallows, "The Passionless Presidency," *The Atlantic*, vol. 244 (May 1979), pp. 33-48, was one of the first to point out how much the lack of Washington connections affected the Carter administration. According to Fallows, this lack of connections, when combined with Carter's insecurity over being from the South, manifested itself in a type of arrogance.

8. James Fallows, "The Passionless Presidency, Part II," *The Atlantic* (June 1979), p. 75.

9. Nicholas Lemman, "How Carter Fails: Taking the Politics Out of Government," *The Washington Monthly* (September 1978), p. 20, suggests that Carter's naval and business experience had the following impact on his managerial mind: "He is a Navy Man, a small business man, a man whose experience is that of taking over a command, being told what the problems are, weighing the alternatives, then making the decision—giving the order, seeing it carried out down the chain."

10. James L. Sundquist, "Jimmy Carter as Public Administrator: An Ap-

praisal at Midterm," *Public Administration Review*, vol. 39 (January/February 1979), p. 7.

11. Lemman, "How Carter Fails," p. 14.

12. Bill Moyers, "Carter Interview," *Congressional Quarterly Weekly Report* (November 25, 1978), p. 3358.

13. Presidential News Conference, *Congressional Quarterly Weekly Report* (May 6, 1978), p. 1139.

14. White House Report, "Jordan's New Role Signals an End to 'Cabinet Government,'" *National Journal*, vol. 11 (August 18, 1979), p. 1356.

15. Dom Bonafede, "Carter Sounds Retreat from Cabinet Government," *National Journal Reprint Series* (November 18, 1978).

16. White House Report, "The Power Vacuum Outside the Oval Office," *National Journal*, vol. 10 (February 24, 1978), p. 657.

17. Bonafede, "Carter Sounds Retreat," p. 1356.

18. Ibid., p. 1358.

19. Nathan, *The Plot That Failed*, pp. 45-47.

20. Cited in Sundquist, "Jimmy Carter as Public Administrator," p. 7.

21. Ibid., p. 5.

22. It is here that the overlap between types of management techniques becomes most obvious. The Carter Civil Service Reforms were proposed by the president's reorganization staff and achieved through a reorganization plan. They are included in the discussion on personnel because personnel is the area in which the reforms' impact will be most immediately felt.

23. Ann Cooper, "Congress Approves Civil Service Reforms," *Congressional Quarterly Weekly Report* (October 14, 1973), p. 2945.

24. News Conference Text, (May 8, 1978), *Congressional Quarterly Weekly Report* (May 20, 1978), p. 1272.

25. News Conference Text, (July 20, 1978), *Congressional Quarterly Weekly Report* (July 29, 1978), p. 1972.

26. Naomi B. Lynn and Richard Evaden, "Bureaucratic Responses to Civil Service Reform," *Public Administration Review*, vol. 38 (July/August 1979), p. 333.

27. Leonard Reed, "The Bureaucracy: The Cleverest Lobby of Them All," *The Washington Monthly* (April 1978), p. 49.

28. Dom Bonafede, "White House Reorganization—Separating Smoke from Substance," *National Journal*, vol. 9 (August 20, 1977), p. 1307.

29. Ibid.

30. James G. Benze, Jr., "Presidential Reorganization as a Tactical Weapon," *Presidential Studies Quarterly*, vol. 15 (Winter 1986).

31. The Domestic Council never really fulfilled the expectations of its supporters in the Nixon and Ford administrations. In fact, as Dom Bon-

afede, "White House Reorganization," p. 1310, suggests, the Domestic Council so disappointed its supporters that during the Ford administration, it fell into almost total disuse.

32. As Rochelle Stanfield, "The Reorganization Staff is Big Loser in the Latest Shuffle," *National Journal*, vol. 11 (March 10, 1979), p. 398, points out, one of the unusual aspects of the Carter reorganization efforts is that the responsibility for development of the reorganization plans originated in the Office of Management and Budget. Presidents have generally relied on task forces for their reorganization plans.

33. Rochelle Stanfield, "The Best Laid Reorganization Plans Sometimes Go Astray," *National Journal*, vol. 11 (January 20, 1979), p. 84.

34. Ibid., p. 87.

35. Rochelle Stanfield, "At Least It Didn't Cost Much," *National Journal*, vol. 11 (June 2, 1979), p. 917.

36. Joel Havemann, "Carter's Reorganization Plans—Scrambling for Turf," *National Journal*, vol. 10 (May 20, 1978), p. 791.

37. There are other possible explanations for the ease of the energy reorganization. The energy field tends to be dominated by several large interests, and it is possible that they did not oppose the reorganization because it would be to their advantage to have one government institution in charge of energy policy. It is also possible that the "crisis" aspects of energy policy have given the president greater authority to act in this area.

38. Allen Schick, "The Battle of the Budget," in *Congress Against the Presidency*, ed. Harvey C. Mansfield (New York: Praeger, 1975), pp. 51-70.

39. Joel Havermann, "Taking Up the Tools to Tame the Bureaucracy: Zero Base Budgeting and Sunset Legislation," *National Journal Reprint Series* (November 18, 1978).

40. Allen Schick, "The Road from ZBB," *Public Administration Review*, vol. 38 (March/April 1978), p. 177.

41. As Schick suggests in "The Road from ZBB," there was a compelling political explanation for this budgetary standoff. Committed to fiscal prudence and still cherishing budgetary balance at the end of his first term, President Carter could not afford costly program starts. However, because of the demands for greater spending in behalf of Democratic programs, Carter attempted what his Republican predecessors failed to accomplish. So the Carter budgets neither gave nor took; they simply held the line.

42. James P. Pfiffer, "Budgeting and the 'People's Reform,'" *Public Administration Review*, vol. 40 (March/April 1980), pp. 194-200.

43. Schick, "The Road from ZBB," p. 177.

5
Management in the Reagan Administration

There is a public administration view that you should remove politics from government. I think that's kind of a dream. Politics doesn't of necessity mean partisanship; it simply means that there must be response to what elected officials of government want.[1]

Donald J. Devine
former director of the Office of Personnel Management

THE REAGAN MANAGEMENT STYLE

The management style of Ronald Reagan provides an ideal comparison with that of Jimmy Carter. While the Carter management style can be described as the administration of politics, the Reagan management style can be described as the politics of administration. The Carter style relied heavily on management techniques; the Reagan style depends on political power and influence. As such, the Reagan administration represents a departure from the structural and procedural management initiatives of recent presidential administrations.

This departure has two key characteristics. First, the Reagan administration makes minimal use of the management programs (such as budgeting techniques, policy analysis, or large-scale reorganizations) that have been the mainstay of presidential management. Instead, there has been an increase in the use of more "political" tools, such as White House control over the appointment process, deregulation, and further politicalization of the budget process. It seems that the Reagan administration decided early to abandon the trend toward management by technique in favor of presidential power. As the quotation from Donald J. Devine, Reagan's first director of the Office of Personnel and Management, illustrates, the White House has chosen to "break out" of the politics/administration dichotomy that while thoroughly discredited intellectually, continued to dominate the management programs of recent presidents.[2]

Many of the Reagan administration's specific strategies are in fact not new. For example, the Nixon administration placed a heavy emphasis on controlling the personnel appointment process, and the Ford and Carter administrations attempted deregulation. The difference between the Reagan administration and previous administrations is the shift in focus. The Reagan administration places less emphasis on increased efficiency and/or economy, and more on presidential control to ensure enactment of the president's programs. The Reagan emphasis is perhaps most evident in the administration's approach to personnel.

PERSONNEL

Ronald Reagan is the first modern president to fully recognize that the presidential power of appointment may be the key to controlling policy implementation. No president in recent memory has placed an equivalent effort into appointing key personnel in cabinet and subcabinet positions. Reagan's transition team realized that the success of the administration program would ultimately depend on controlling the appointment process. Control necessitated central clearance by Reagan loyalists, meaning oversight of Reagan appointees by members of the White House staff.[3]

Even before the election, as part of the transition plan, Edwin Meese asked E. Pendleton James to put together a plan for presidential control of the appointment process, which required the development of job descriptions, lists of qualified candidates, and so on to be given to cabinet secretaries. Also needed was a thorough screening process involving both the Reagan kitchen cabinet and the triumvirate of Edwin Meese, James A. Baker III, and Michael Deaver checking the candidates' political qualifications. In this administration, however, political qualifications meant less than generally accepted political connections, but rather their loyalty to Ronald Reagan and their credentials as Reagan conservatives. The Reagan advisors had only two important questions: Was the appointee a Reagan loyalist (generally defined as having worked in the campaign)? Was the appointee a Reagan conservative? While previous presidents demanded loyalty from top-level cabinet officials (remember Carter dismissed Health, Education, and Welfare Secretary Joseph Califano for perceived disloyalty), the Reagan administration emphasized loyalty from subcabinet officials as well and added the criterion of ideological purity. Far distant in importance for appointment were integrity, competence, and prior experience.

Interestingly, some of the initial appointees were criticized as being merely Nixon and Ford retreads, rather than true Reaganites. However, as the appointment process progressed, the conservative nature of the appointees—particularly those appointed agency heads, regulatory commissioners, and members of the subcabinet—became evident. As G. Calvin MacKenzie noted, "Reagan's economic policy appointments were all card carrying supplysiders. His foreign and defense policy appointees shared a world view founded on a deep skepticism of the motives of the Soviet Union. His choices in social and health policy positions were uniformly 'pro life' and 'pro family' in their orientation. . . . "[4] At the most crucial operating level of the federal government, the Reagan White House has been successful in appointing individuals with deep and abiding loyalties to Ronald Reagan and his programs and no real commitment to past programs and policies.

The importance of the personnel process to the Reagan White House can also be illustrated organizationally. E. Pendleton James was the first modern presidential personnel director to rank at an Executive Level III position and the first to have an office in the West Wing of the White House. Even more important, James was made a member of the senior staff and had regular access to the president, making it impossible for cabinet officials to subvert the established personnel procedures with "end runs" to the president on behalf of favored appointees.[5]

However, central clearance of the appointment process created additional problems. Because groups that supported Reagan during the 1980 campaign did not participate in the process, these supporters were disgruntled with their lack of political spoils. Better communication in the future might help alleviate this problem. A more serious problem was the glacial pace with which the appointment process moved. At the end of Reagan's first four months, only 55 percent of the top four hundred officials had been announced and only 36 percent formally nominated, with only 21 percent confirmed.[6] To a certain extent, this difficulty may have been beyond the administration's control. The more extensive reporting requirements of the newly adopted Ethics in Government Act slowed the appointment process, as did the administration's immediate focus on passage of the Economic Recovery Tax Act.[7] However, the easiest way to speed up the appointment process would have been to follow the Carter administration's example and decentralize personnel decisions to cabinet secretaries. For obvious reasons, this is the one thing the administration could not do, and thus paid the consequences with difficulty in meeting appointment deadlines.

The centralization of the personnel process also resulted in the appointment of inexperienced managers, whose political and administrative naïveté may have done the administration more harm than good (James Watt and Anne Burford being obvious examples). Finally, Reagan appointees have also had difficulty in establishing working relationships with the career civil service in their departments and agencies. Such problems in Health and Human Services and the Justice Department have reportedly affected professionalism and retention among the department civil servants.[8]

At the same time the president has sought to control the appointment process, he has waged a battle against the permanent bureaucracy through hiring freezes, reductions in force, and reductions in salaries.[9] The administration has also used the centerpiece of the Carter personnel program—the Senior Executive Service (SES)—to its own advantage. One of the rationales for SES was that it would provide the president and his political appointees greater control over the top-level managers in the career civil service. There is considerable evidence that the Reagan administration has used SES to accomplish this goal. Dick Kirschen reports on a draft memorandum signed by Edwin Meese, Donald J. Devine, and Deputy Office of Management and Budget Director Joseph R. Wright, uncovered by Representative Patricia Schroeder, that "addressed to the heads of departments and agencies . . . , asserted that personnel performance appraisals could be used as an important vehicle to insure that administration initiatives and policies are appropriately carried out and that the primary objectives of the President are accomplished."[10]

The Reagan administration has also made liberal use of a provision in the 1978 Civil Service Reform Act that allows a political appointee to reassign career officials to other departments or agencies after 120 days. While some of the transfers have undoubtedly been for other than political purposes, some obviously have been made for just such a reason. Bernard Rosen suggests that "some highly publicized reassignments . . . after the change in administrations leaves one with a very uneasy feeling about the use and possible abuse of the reassignment power. . . . We can reasonably assume that abuse of this power or the fear of abuse would have a paralyzing effect on initiative and candor."[11] While Rosen is surely correct in arguing the disastrous implications of SES, the system seems to be operating as originally designed. Therefore, the more important question concerns the seeming incompatibility of increased presidential control of the civil service and the principles of a merit system.

While the White House has been enthusiastic about greater presidential control of the career civil service, the bureaucratic view is radically different. By all accounts, morale among SES members is very low. Of three hundred career executives surveyed by the Federal Institute Alumni Association, 44 percent said the creation of SES has had a negative impact on management efficiency and effectiveness; 40 percent said it had no effect; and only 16 percent said it impacted favorably. Moreover, 61 percent thought that its impact on political appointee–career executive relations has been negative.[12] Retention has also become a problem—about 95 percent of top bureaucrats reaching retirement age are deciding to leave, compared with about 18 percent in 1978.[13] Thus, while the SES system may have increased presidential power in the short run, its long-term effect may be somewhat different for an executive branch facing the loss of many experienced managers.

CABINET COUNCILS

One of the continuing myths of new presidential administrations seems to be the importance of cabinet government. Every recent administration has entered the White House singing the praises of cabinet government. The Nixon and Carter administrations both pledged to make the cabinet an important decision making institution. However, the lure of cabinet government soon gave way to the pressures of the political process, and decision making came to be dominated by the White House staff. For example, few can remember the name of Richard Nixon's secretary of state, but everyone remembers his national security advisor, Henry Kissinger.[14]

The Reagan administration also initially made a commitment to cabinet government. In fact, the administration attempted to develop an institutional structure that would routinize cabinet participation in executive branch decision making—cabinet councils. Originally the pet project of Presidential Counselor Edwin Meese, the five cabinet councils were Commerce and Trade (CCCT), Economic Affairs (CCEA), Food and Agriculture (CCFA), Human Resources (CCHR), and Natural Resources and Environment (CCNRE). Councils on Legal Affairs and Management (CCLAM) and Administration were added later.

Each cabinet council consisted of six to ten cabinet secretaries and the heads of relevant agencies from the Executive Office of the President (EOP). The councils were to bring the cabinet into the decision-making process by interfacing cabinet officers with EOP officials and to attempt to prevent cabinet conflict when any policy overlaps two or more departments.

Early in the administration, the cabinet councils' general level of activity seemed to ensure they would play a prominent role in decision making. From February 1981 to mid-May 1982, a total of 190 council meetings were held. However, the meetings were not evenly distributed among all the councils. Over 100 of the 190 meetings can be attributed to the Cabinet Council on Economic Affairs (52 percent), three times the number of the next most active council—Commerce and Trade, which met 31 times. The other cabinet councils met even less: Human Resources, 15; Natural Resources and Environment, 11; Food and Agriculture, 10; and Legal Policy (added later), 3.[15] At least part of the disparity in meeting is undoubtedly due to the heavy emphasis on economic policy early in the Reagan first term.

Attendance figures at the cabinet council meetings indicate the meetings were taken seriously by the cabinet members and at least some of the Executive Office staff. Reagan participated in 14 percent (26) of the meetings; Martin Anderson, 65 percent (124); Murray Weidenbaum, 60 percent (114); Donald Regan, 59 percent (113); Malcolm Baldrige, 53 percent (100); Drew Lewis, 49 percent (93); and Vice President George Bush, 44 percent (88). Interestingly, however, the president's closest advisors were conspicuously absent. For example, Edwin Meese attended 35 meetings (18 percent) and James Baker only 13 meetings (7 percent).[16] Thus, these figures suggest that the cabinet councils have not been successful in bringing together the members of the White House staff and cabinet secretaries.

It is also difficult to conclude that the cabinet councils have brought cabinet members into the decision-making process. Using cabinet council minutes, Chester A. Newland took the number of times the president attended the cabinet council meetings and made a decision on the agenda item there or shortly afterward as a measure of council influence. He reports that decisions were made on 17 of 398 agenda items presented (4 percent). However, because the president attended only 14 percent of the cabinet council meetings, this figure may be somewhat misleading—cabinet council influence could be less direct. A more accurate measure of cabinet council influence may be how many recommendations result in specific presidential action. Newland reports that presidential decision making occurred with about 15 percent of cabinet council agenda items. Some of the more important examples of cabinet council recommendations acted upon by the president include: CCEA = the Cancun Summit, and Employment and Training Policy; CCCT = Maritime Policy; CCHR = Pro-Competition Health Care Proposals; CCNRE = Natural Gas Decontrol; and CCFA = Surplus Cheese Disposal and Sugar Policy.[17]

However, not all policy decisions are created equal. Therefore, it is important to consider the cabinet councils' level of impact on the Reagan administration's major (as well as minor) decisions. With this criterion, the picture is somewhat different. Certainly, the major domestic policy initiative of Reagan's first term was the Economic Recovery Tax Act. There is little doubt that credit for the economic package must be given to Budget Director David Stockman and the Office of Management and Budget staff. By the time the cabinet councils were formed, most of the economic program was already developed, with often less than enthusiastic cabinet support. In fact, for most of the first term, many of the most important policy decisions were reportedly made in Chief of Staff James Baker's office, during "legislative strategy" sessions. These meetings were very exclusive and rarely included cabinet members.[18]

The same pattern seems to be emerging in Reagan's second term. For example, the changes in the president's tax reform package were not even discussed in the Economic Affairs Council. Instead, they were developed in a much smaller ad hoc group with only four active participants: Chief of Staff Donald Regan; Treasury Secretary James Baker; his executive secretary, Richard G. Darman; and Assistant Treasury Secretary Ronald A. Pearlman (Vice President Bush and White House aides Patrick Buchanan, Alfred H. Kingon, and David L. Chew were also present, but less active).[19] Conspicuous by their absence were Chairman of the Council of Economic Advisors Beryl W. Sprinkel, Budget Director David Stockman, and Commerce Secretary Malcolm Baldrige.

It is unclear, then, exactly what the administration means by cabinet government. It is true that through the cabinet council system, the administration has developed a process for institutionalizing the involvement of the cabinet in routine decisions. However, as a group, the cabinet has not penetrated to the heart of presidential decision making. On those matters most important to the administration, decisions are made by White House staff members, with participation by select members of the inner cabinet (Defense, Treasury, State, and Justice). In this regard, the Reagan administration differs very little from previous administrations. As already discussed, cabinet officers have little input into the personnel process, which has also been centralized in the White House office. Is this cabinet government? Decentralization of decision making may run from the president to his inner circle of advisors, but on important decisions, it does not extend to the cabinet.

DEREGULATION

The most controversial Reagan administrative effort has been the movement toward deregulation. For several reasons, the administration feels that deregulation is not only beneficial but almost mandatory. First, many of the president's economic advisors (notably

Murray Weidenbaum and David Stockman) argued that costs associated with deregulation were a contributing factor in the economic
debacle inherited from the Carter administration. Stockman, in his
now-famous Dunkirk memo, forcibly stated this position:

A dramatic, substantial recession of the regulatory burden is needed for
the short term cash flow relief it will provide to business firms and the
long term signal it will provide to corporate investment planners. A major
"regulatory ventilation" will do much to boost business confidence and
fiscal tax measures.[20]

However, the Reagan commitment to deregulation stems from
more than economic necessity. It is also an article of ideological
faith. Most of the Reagan team viewed government as too large, too
unwieldy, too powerful, and too meddlesome. Their vow was to get
government "off the backs and out of the pockets" of private citizens, small businesses, and large corporations. Deregulation was
one of the tools to be used in this herculean task.

While deregulation is commonly assumed to have originated with
Ronald Reagan, deregulation efforts can be traced at least as far
back as the Nixon administration. Under Nixon, the Office of Management and Budget (OMB) initiated "quality of life" reviews, aimed
in theory at all agencies having regulatory power over occupational
safety and environmental and consumer protection. In practice,
however, most of the regulations reviewed were from the Environmental Protection Agency. President Ford required the Council on
Wage and Price Stability to use inflation impact statements to assess
the inflationary impact of various federal programs. However, because its review power was operative only after agency decision
making was complete, the administration could only offer a public
critique in the hope of generating either congressional or media
interest.[21]

Carter also was interested in deregulation. He issued Executive
Order 12,044 that required each agency to create a semiannual
agenda of "significant regulations" currently under agency development, to initiate early presidential involvement. The order also
required agencies to review existing rules in order to assess the
need for changes or elimination; major rules (those with an economic impact of $100 million or more) were to be analyzed for

alternatives and cost-effectiveness. Finally, the order created the Regulatory Advisory Review Group and the Regulatory Council to enforce regulatory guidelines. While evaluations of Carter's success with deregulation are mixed, Executive Order 12,044 is attributed with having "substantially broadened both the scope and the impact of central regulatory clearance on behalf of the President."[22] Thus, the stage was set for an activist president committed to regulatory relief.

The Reagan administration came to Washington in 1980 ready to launch a broad-based attack on the regulatory process. On January 28, 1981, Reagan suspended nearly two hundred "midnight regulations" enacted by the Carter administration until their economic impact could be reviewed. Two days after taking office, Reagan commissioned a cabinet-level Task Force on Regulatory Relief, chaired by Vice President Bush. The task force was given the power to review the regulatory proposals of all executive branch agencies. Less than a month later, Reagan issued Executive Order 12,291, giving the Director of OMB, operating under the direction of the task force, central clearance authority for the regulatory process. Under the order, each executive branch agency must submit proposed rules to OMB for review. After review, OMB is empowered to withhold publication of the rules until the agency responds to OMB's comments but cannot ultimately stop the agency from publishing the rules. It can only refer the regulations in question to the regulatory task force. Particularly important is the requirement that regulatory action cannot be taken unless the potential benefits of a given rule outweigh the potential costs. Thus, the Reagan executive order addressed the issue of cost–benefit analysis skirted by the Carter executive order. Murray Weidenbaum, head of the President's Council of Economic Advisors, made the following case for cost–benefit analysis.

The potential benefits to society of implementing the regulatory action must outweigh the potential costs. While this seems straightforward enough, it is actually a critical and highly sophisticated point. No longer will we tolerate the view that economic issues are necessarily on a lower rung of the ethical ladder than some regulatory issue.[23]

Within OMB, primary responsibility for oversight of the cost–benefit analysis fell to the Office of Information and Regulatory Affairs (OIRA).

While Executive Order 12,291 included new and existing rules of all types, emphasis was again on "major" rules—those with an annual economic impact of $100 million or more. Agencies that propose major rules are required to develop a Regulatory Impact Analysis (RIA) unless exempted by OMB. RIAs are essentially cost–benefit analyses, listing not only benefits and costs with a summary of net benefits but also possible alternatives with their benefits and costs.

Robert Gilmour has summarized the statistical impact of central regulatory clearance. In the first two years of the program, most of the rules reviewed by OMB were nonmajor (97 percent of 2,446 rules in 1981 and 96 percent of 2,633 rules in 1982). In 1981, 90 percent of the total number of proposed and final rules were approved by OMB as submitted. In 1982, 84 percent of the rules were also approved as submitted. Only 87 of the 2,633 rules submitted in 1982 were either returned unapproved or withdrawn. In 1981, 60 major rules were submitted (22 with RIAs), and in 1983, 80 major rules were submitted (41 with RIAs).[24] The Task Force on Regulatory Relief considered 91 rules and 9 paperwork requirements during the same time period, convincing agencies to change or kill 37 rules.[25]

Some of the more important deregulatory successes during the first year included the following:

- The National Highway Traffic Safety Administration revised or killed twelve rules, the most important rules concerning relief from 1985 fuel economy standards and the installation of passive restraints.
- The Agriculture Department changed the labeling and marketing of deboned meat (including more bone fragments). Estimated savings—$495 million.
- The Education Department killed rules requiring bilingual education. Estimated savings for local school districts—$1 billion.
- The Labor Department proposed trimming the prevailing wage requirements that govern salaries paid by government contractors.[26]

However, it has been difficult for the Reagan administration to sustain its initial success in deregulation. As the result of a number of lawsuits, the federal courts have overturned several deregulatory decisions. For example, the *State Farm Automobile Company v. the Department of Transportation*, the U.S. Court of Appeals for the District of Columbia overturned the Transportation Department's recession of the Carter administration's requirement that automobiles be equipped with passive restraint systems such as air bags. The court ruled that the decision was "arbitrary and capricious," while establishing that agencies could not repeal well-established rules without in-depth documentation.[27]

There have also been repeated charges that Executive Order 12,291 may be illegal (although not yet challenged on this grounds) and if not illegal, certainly responsible for a politicalization of the administrative rule-making process. The charge of illegality stems from its supposed violation of the Administrative Procedures Act of 1946. Critics argue that the act places rule-making authority only in the hands of agency heads, and not OMB. Moreover, the 1946 act also requires that rule-making be based solely on information in an agency's public record. The secret nature of OMB deliberations is charged with violating the spirit and the letter of this act.

Critics also charge that the secretive nature of OMB's review process is an open invitation to influence peddling. The following exchange between Representative Albert Gore, Jr. (D, Tenn.), and James C. Miller (then head of OIRA) at a congressional hearing illustrates their concerns.

Gore: When you met with the Chemical Manufacturers Association on February 23 of this year and discussed their "support for regulatory relief," isn't there just a chance they mentioned the hazardous waste disposal regulations which were ordered to be reviewed by your task force just 30 days later?

Miller: No.

Gore: What about February 18, 1981? You met with the American Mining Congress and discussed support for regulatory relief. Isn't it more likely that you discussed their support for the postponement of the Interior Department's rule on the extraction of coal, which has now been postponed indefinitely?

Miller: I cannot recall that meeting.[28]

A list of meetings that OMB supplied to the House Oversight and Investigations Subcommittee in April 1981 detailed thirty-six meetings held by OMB officials with business and consumer groups over a two-month period. Of the thirty-six meetings, all but four were with major industries or their lobbyists, ranging from the Chamber of Commerce to the Garbage Compactor Manufacturers Association (they discussed noise standards).[29]

Critics of Executive Order 12,291 have also questioned its success in devising an institutional process for regulatory relief. Some point out that OMB's staff, consisting of less than ninety people who are responsible for regulatory clearance for all the executive branch, is just too small for the task at hand. The statistics cited earlier illustrate this point. In 1981, over 90 percent of proposed rules passed OMB review without comment. In 1982, the figure was 96 percent. Given the number of regulations involved (2,446 in 1981 and 2,633 in 1982), OIRA's overall impact must be considered fairly minimal. It might also be pointed out that OIRA is currently operating with $4.5 million less in budget allocation than was given to equivalent agencies under Carter. The result may be that OIRA will have to increasingly rely on agency evaluations instead of their own. If so, cost–benefit analysis is unlikely to work.

In fact, it may be that the Reagan administration's deregulation efforts will not be achieved through Executive Order 12,291 but rather through its focus on personnel and budgets. Even cursory examination of some of Ronald Reagan's key appointees suggests that die-hard deregulators (generally lawyers who have made a career of fighting liberal activity over the regulatory policy of Congress) have been positioned very carefully in the federal bureaucracy. There was, of course, James Watt, the former secretary of the interior who before assuming office headed a conservative public interest law firm that battled on behalf of developers. Or there is Raymond A. Peck, appointed to head the National Highway Safety Council with little background in highway safety but lots of experience in fighting for deregulation of the auto industry. In addition, Reagan appointees now govern the Federal Trade Commission, the Federal Communications Commission, and the National Labor Relations Board. Importantly, unlike cabinet secretaries, the appointees to regulatory boards do not automatically disappear when a new president takes office. They are there until their terms expire.[30] Once again, the administration has shrewdly deduced the importance of filling key positions in the federal bureaucracy with appointees committed to the Reagan agenda.

The deregulation effort demonstrates the intensely political nature of the Reagan administrative program. Executive Order 12,291 intentionally politicizes the administrative rule-making procedure, as developed under the Administrative Procedures Act of 1946, in pursuit of accomplishing through administration what cannot be gained legislatively. However, if that effort proves unsuccessful (and current evidence indicates a strong possibility that this may occur), deregulation has and will continue to occur through presidential control of the appointment process. Clearly, in this presidency, the distinction between politics and administration has virtually disappeared.

BUDGETING

No area of administration more graphically illustrates the differing management styles of Presidents Carter and Reagan than their approach to budgeting. Carter attempted to gain control over the budget process through the use of a specific management technique—zero base budgeting—thus fitting squarely into a decade-and-a-half trend of presidential budgeting. What is unique about the Reagan administration is that it has abandoned budgeting techniques as a method of gaining influence in the budget process. Instead, it has focused on controlling budget expenditures through the exercise of presidential power and influence. In this sense, deregulation and budgeting are opposite sides of the same coin—efforts to trim the activities of a wasteful, bloated, meddling federal bureaucracy. This goal would only be accomplished through the two-pronged attack of deregulation and budget cuts. David Stockman, director of the Office of Management and Budget and architect of the Reagan budget cuts, noted the importance of the cuts to Reagan supply-siders.

Deep down in his soul, Phil Gramm was a hard core anti-spender. In his mind, as in mine, the first principles of the anti-statist revolution were complementary. They required an enormous shrinkage of the vast expenditures that the Congress pumped into illicit and inappropriate functions of the state. That permitted lower taxes that necessitated far less spending. So Phil and I thought of ourselves as the complete supplysiders. We wanted to shrink both sides of the budget equation. The economic and political circumstances of early 1980 gave us a chance to try just that.[31]

And of the welcome opportunity afforded them early in the Reagan first term:

At the time, the prospect of needing well over $100 billion in domestic cuts to keep the Republican budget in equilibrium appeared more as an opportunity than as a roadblock. Once Governor Reagan got an electoral mandate for Kemp-Roth and 10-5-3, then we would have the second Republic's craven politicians pinned to the wall. They would have to dismantle its bloated, wasteful, and unjust spending enterprises—or risk national ruin.[32]

The desire to reverse the seemingly inevitable growth of the federal budget was evident in the president's five-year budget plan, contained in the Program for Economic Recovery. While providing for a larger defense buildup than proposed by Carter, the plan proposed by OMB (now completely transformed into a political arm of the White House office) called for a balanced budget by 1984—even in the face of huge losses in tax revenues. This obviously created the impetus for very large domestic budget cuts. According to the plan, reductions in nondefense spending for 1982 would total $40 billion, and by 1986, would grow to $400 billion. The targeted cuts ranged from about 2 percent for transportation to over 60 percent for employment and training.[33]

These are not the type of spending reductions likely to be brought about by new budgeting techniques. Budget cuts of this size depended upon the exercise of presidential power and influence. Even within the administration, political maneuvering was necessary. To get the budget cuts through the cabinet, Stockman created the budget working group, where cabinet secretaries, accompanied by career civil service advisors (because of delays in the appointment process, their political appointees were not yet in place), faced a brutal interrogation by Stockman, Martin Anderson, and Murray Weidenbaum. Stockman and his colleagues were so successful (within two weeks they had achieved 90 percent of their cuts) that the room in which they met came to be called the cutting room.[34]

However, pushing the cuts through the administration was only the first step. They still had to be pushed through Congress, especially the Democratic-controlled House of Representatives. The administration had several advantages in this effort. Even though the House of Representatives was controlled by Democrats, the president had a natural group of allies in southern Democrats (boll weevils). Second, the Reagan administration had a firm ally on the House Budget Committee in Phil Gramm who, with Stockman, planned a clever strategy in confronting the House leadership. Third, the administration was not averse to cutting political deals to swing reluctant supporters into line. For example, $400 million in Veterans Administration's health-care cuts were restored in order to attract the support of Sonny Montgomery, one of the leaders of the boll weevils.[35] Fourth, and perhaps most important, at this stage the Stockman cuts still had the support of the president, who used his considerable rhetorical talents and personal influence to help sell the program.

However, the first round of cuts, difficult as they were to sell, only marked the beginning. As revenues fell as a result of tax cuts and dramatic reductions in inflation, the budget deficit grew larger, requiring a second, even larger round of cuts. At this point, according to Stockman, the administration lost its nerve. It ruled entitlement programs off limits and refused to consider new taxes to increase government revenues. Without either new taxes or budget cuts, ever-increasing budget deficits were inevitable, especially in light of declining rates of economic growth. Perhaps it is true, as Stockman and others claim, that the president and his closest advisors never fully grasped the enormity of their task, and therefore missed a unique opportunity to enact the revolutionary supply-side agenda.

However, to assume failure on the part of the administration overlooks some obvious impacts of the budget cuts. Specifically, the administration has been successful in restricting agency activities by limiting expenditures. A report by the Center for the Study of American Business at Washington University (St. Louis, Mo.) showed that agency budgets were trimmed by 8 percent during Reagan's first term and, as a result, agency staffing declined by 10 percent. Regulatory agencies were hit particularly hard. The fiscal 1982 budget proposed cutting the Environmental Protection Agency's budget by $90 million, the Consumer Product Safety Commission by $14 million, and the Federal Trade Commission by $8 million.[36] As a result, the OMB proposed staff cuts of 25 to 30 percent for these agencies. Obviously, with less funds and fewer staff, the agencies' regulatory and oversight capacities would suffer and "back door" regulatory relief takes place. The federal government has not been put out of the regulatory business, but regulatory agencies' ability to perform its function has been diminished. Thus, the Reagan administration has been able to accomplish through budget cuts what has been impossible through the legislative process.

In the first term, the Reagan administration also changed the nature of the budget debate. Where previously the budget process had focused on levels of increase in domestic programs, through the first Reagan term the debate centered on how much and where the budget should be cut. As a result, new programs and increased funding for existing programs rarely even made it onto the congressional agenda. Current increases in government spending are driven primarily by increases in defense spending and automatic increases in entitlement programs (particularly Social Security and Medicare). Thus, in just four short years, there occurred a radical change in the budget process. Through the shrewd use of political influence, excellent timing, and the leadership of a popular president (not through budgeting techniques), the world of the federal budget has been a very different place.

SUMMARY

The most interesting feature of Reagan's management style has been the effort to accomplish administrative objectives through political maneuvers. For example, one of the administration's major objectives has been regulatory relief. While it is true that they have developed an administrative process for deregulation (as contained in Executive Order 12,291), the commitment of administrative resources to this effort has been minimal and the degree of success marginal. However, this does not mean that regulatory relief has not occurred. Strategic use of political appointees and the exercise of presidential influence in the budget process have provided regulatory relief through nonenforcement.

The benefit of such a process is obvious: immediate regulatory relief. Changing regulatory laws or modifying the administrative process is time-consuming and involves a large expenditure of political capital. Nonenforcement can be done immediately with minimal drain on the administration's limited political resources. However, what may not be immediately apparent is that such change is not likely to be permanent. Eventually, political appointees move on and budget cuts can be restored. If neither the law nor the administrative process has changed, deregulation is likely to be short-lived. Thus, while the Reagan administration's management style seems successful, it might also prove to be temporary.

NOTES

1. Dick Kirschten, "Administration Using Carter-Era Reform to Manipulate the Levers of Government," *National Journal*, vol. 15 (April 19, 1983), p. 133.

2. Laurence E. Lynn, Jr., "Manager's Role in Public Management," *The Bureaucrat*, vol. 13 (Winter 1984), pp. 21–22. Lynn provides an excellent discussion about why, despite criticism, the politics/administration dichotomy continues to be used.

3. G. Calvin MacKenzie, "Personnel Selection for a Conservative Administration: The Reagan Experience, 1980–81," unpublished paper, and G. Calvin MacKenzie, "Cabinet and Subcabinet Personnel Selections in Reagan's First Year: New Variations on Some Not-So-Old Themes," paper presented at the Annual Meeting of the American Political Science Association, New York City (September 2–5, 1982), provide an excellent look at the personnel process in the Reagan administration.

4. MacKenzie, "Personnel Selection for a Conservative Administration," p. 4.

5. Ibid., p. 6.

6. Chester A. Newland, "The Reagan Presidency: Limited Government and Political Administration," *Public Administration Review*, vol. 43 (January/February 1983), p. 6.

7. In fact, the lack of appointees in key positions may have helped the development of the program because of a corresponding lack of bureaucratic resistance. Some have gone so far as to suggest it was a deliberate strategy.

8. Linda E. Demkovich, "Team Player Schweiker May Be Paying a High Price for His Loyalty to Reagan," *National Journal*, vol. 15 (May 15, 1982), p. 848.

9. Dick Kirschten, "Reagan Gets Unsolicited Advice on His Personnel Appointments," *National Journal*, vol. 17 (December 14, 1985), p. 2868.

10. Dick Kirschten, "Administration Using Carter-Era Reform to Manipulate the Levers of Government," p. 733.

11. Bernard Rosen, "A Disaster for Merit," *The Bureaucrat*, vol. 11 (Winter 1982–83), pp. 11–13.

12. William J. Lanouette, "SES—From Civil Service Showpiece to Incipient Failure in Two Years," *National Journal*, vol. 13 (July 18, 1981), p. 1296.

13. Ibid.

14. The correct answer is William Rogers.

15. Newland, "The Reagan Presidency," pp. 6–11.

16. Ibid., p. 8.

17. Ibid.

18. Dick Kirschten, "Reagan's Cabinet Councils May Have Less Influence Than Meets the Eye," *National Journal*, vol. 13 (July 11, 1981), p. 1246.

19. Dick Kirschten, "Once Again Cabinet Government's Beauty . . . Lies in Being No More Than Skin Deep," *National Journal*, vol. 17 (June 15, 1985), p. 1418.

20. Quoted in John L. Palmer and Isabel V. Sawhill, eds., *The Reagan Experiment* (Washington, D.C.: Urban Institute Press, 1982), p. 131.

21. Robert S. Gilmour, "Controlling Regulation in the Reagan Administration: The Emergence of Central Clearance," paper presented at the Annual Conference of the New England Political Science Association, U.S. Naval War College, Newport, R. I. (April 13, 1984), p. 4.

22. Ibid., p. 5.

23. Quoted in Timothy B. Clark, "Do the Benefits Justify the Costs? Prove It, Says the Administration," *National Journal*, vol. 13 (August 1, 1981), p. 1382.

24. Gilmour, "Controlling Regulation in the Reagan Administration," pp. 5–6.

25. Michael Wines, "Reagan's Reforms Are Full of Sound and Fury, but What Do They Signify?" *National Journal*, vol. 14 (January 16, 1982), pp. 96–97.

26. Ibid.

27. Michael Wines, "Administration, Critics Play Legal Cat and Mouse on Agency Rules," *National Journal*, vol. 14 (December 18, 1982), p. 2159.

28. Michael Wines, "Reagan's Reforms Are Full of Sound and Fury, but What Do They Signify?" p. 95.

29. Ibid.

30. Ann Cooper, "Reagan Has Tamed the Regulatory Beast but Not Permanently Broken Its Grip," *National Journal*, vol. 17 (December 1, 1984), p. 2284.

31. David Stockman, *The Triumph of Politics: Why the Reagan Revolution Failed* (New York: Harper and Row, 1986), p. 52.

32. Ibid., p. 68.

33. John L. Palmer and Gregory B. Mills, "Budget Policy," in *The Reagan Experiment*, ed. John L. Palmer and Isabel V. Sawhill (Washington, D.C.: Urban Institute Press, 1982), pp. 70–72.

34. Stockman, *The Triumph of Politics*, p. 112.

35. Ibid., p. 175.

36. Cooper, "Reagan Has Tamed the Regulatory Beast," p. 2286.

6

An Empirical Investigation of Presidential Management

The desire to maximize presidential control over policy implementation has been a key feature of the Carter and Reagan administrations. They have, however, sought to increase presidential control in very different ways. Carter relied primarily on administrative techniques, while Reagan has relied on presidential influence. The empirical data in this chapter confirms an essential theoretical point of this study: The four-decade trend toward presidential management, based on an administrative model, peaks in the Carter administration. Reagan has adopted a more political model with the same goal of increasing presidential management. The conclusions drawn from the empirical investigation suggest that the emphasis on administrative techniques (especially in the Carter administration) has largely been wasted. According to members of the federal bureaucracy, they have not worked. The conclusion on the Reagan approach is more mixed. Under Reagan, presidential power in the administrative process has increased, but at what cost?

A BRIEF ACCOUNT OF THE RESEARCH

Data for evaluating the management programs were gathered through two mail surveys of executives in administrative positions in the major domestic departments and agencies in the summers of 1980 (the Carter survey) and 1984 (the Reagan survey).[1] The response rates were 47 percent for the Carter administration (450 questionnaires mailed; 212 returned) and 35 percent for the Reagan administration (430 questionnaires mailed; 150 returned).[2] In both surveys, responses were received from all domestic departments and agencies surveyed, and the response samples were representative of the universe.[3]

The response samples for both surveys were dominated by career civil servants—95 percent for the Carter survey and 90 percent for the Reagan survey. A greater mix of political executives and career civil servants was initially sought, but the response pattern is not unrepresentative of the sample. Although both the Carter and Reagan administrations increased the number of political appointees, clearly the majority of administrative positions are filled by career civil servants.

EVALUATING THE EFFECTIVENESS OF PRESIDENTIAL MANAGEMENT: THE CARTER ADMINISTRATION

If recent presidents, and particularly President Jimmy Carter, have been able to gain greater control over policy implementation by using administrative techniques, this control should be reflected in the evaluations of administrative officials. Because of their close association with the implementation of programs and the application of administrative techniques, the officials can provide a firsthand account of presidential management success.

Therefore, in the 1980 survey of presidential management in the Carter administration, administrative officials were asked to evaluate the effectiveness of reorganization, staffing, political appointees, transfers, and budgeting on a scale of 1 (very effective) through 5 (not very effective). Table 3 summarizes the results in percentages of positive and negative evaluations of the effectiveness of the techniques as tools of presidential management.[4]

This table reveals some surprises. The effectiveness of two of the administrative techniques (reorganization and transfers) was evaluated negatively. Staffing, political appointees, and budgeting were evaluated positively, as effective tools of presidential management.

The negative evaluation of reorganization is surprising, given the heavy emphasis presidents have placed on reorganization as a man-

Table 3
Effectiveness of Management Techniques

Administrative Technique	Percent Positive Evaluation	Percent Negative Evaluation
Reorganization	31	42
Staffing	44	32
Political appointees	64	18
Transfers	33	42
Budgeting	65	18

agement tool. Even though presidents have consistently used reorganization to gain greater control over policy implementation, career bureaucrats obviously do not consider reorganization to be particularly effective.

The positive evaluation of budgeting (65 percent) is also surprising, since the literature generally suggests that budgeting techniques have had limited success in increasing presidential power because of bureaucratic resistance in incorporating the techniques into agency budget programs. However, the positive evaluation may represent a general evaluation of the president's role in the budget process rather than an evaluation of a particular budgeting technique.[5] Evaluations of zero base budgeting in the Carter administration (discussed later in this chapter) illustrate this point.

The administrative officials also considered staffing to be moderately effective. Their evaluation may represent acceptance of the White House staff as a management tool. This acceptance would not be unexpected, given that presidents as different as Franklin Roosevelt and Richard Nixon used their staffs in oversight capacities.

The administrative executives would also be expected to perceive political appointees as an effective tool of presidential management. Because of the importance of political appointees to presidential management, administrative executives were asked to identify the proper (ideal) role for political appointees and their actual role, choosing from the following roles: advocate of the president's interests, neutral administrator, advocate of the agency's interests, and advocate of the constituency's interests.

Table 4 summarizes the executives' perceptions of political appointees' roles. The responses indicate a surprising degree of acceptance of political appointees as advocates of the president's interests (84 percent). In fact, the two sets of responses suggest that bureaucrats might be willing to accept an increase in the political appointees' actual role as the president's advocate. The responses in the second column indicate that the administrative executives, like presidents, feel that political appointees run the risk of becoming captives of agency or constituency interests.

Data were also gathered on the application of administrative techniques in the Carter administration. The officials were asked to identify the degree to which the Carter administration used reorganization, staffing, political appointees, transfers, the Senior Executive Service (SES), and zero base budgeting (ZBB) to increase presidential control. Table 5 summarizes the results of this investigation. As indicated in the table, budgeting (67 percent) and reorganization (53 percent) were considered to be key parts of the management program, confirming the overview of the Carter man-

Table 4
Role of Political Appointees I

Role	Percent Response Ideal	Percent Response Actual
Advocate of the president's interests	84	59
Neutral administrator	8	4
Advocate of the agency's interests	7	19
Advocate of the constituency's interests	1	19

agement style presented in Chapter 4. The responses also indicate that the Carter White House staff was not perceived as being used as a significant management tool, perhaps reflecting the administration's early emphasis on cabinet government. As expected, personnel transfers also were not identified as a significant part of the management program.

To determine the success of the Carter management efforts, the executives were asked a series of questions directed at specific administrative techniques. For example, the bureaucrats were asked how the Carter administration's reorganization efforts had affected their agency in general and whether the reorganizations had led to improved management in their agency. They were also asked whether the SES had improved management in their agency and whether it provided the president with greater control over career executives. In addition, they were requested to indicate their perception of the oversight capacity of the Carter White House staff and the degree of actual oversight the White House exerted over bureaucratic actions. Finally, the respondents were asked to evaluate the effective-

Table 5
Application of Administrative Techniques in the
Carter Administration

Administrative Technique	Percent of Respondents Feeling Technique Used Frequently	Percent of Respondents Feeling Technique Used Infrequently
Reorganization	53	22
Staffing	25	32
Political appointees	53	26
Transfers	20	64
SES	43	35
ZBB	67	13

ness of ZBB as a management tool and a method for reordering budget priorities.

Table 6 summarizes the executives' answers, using the mean response for each technique as a measure of central tendency. A mean between 1 and 3.5 should be interpreted as tending toward a positive evaluation and a mean between 3.5 and 6 as a negative evaluation.[6] As indicated in the table, the overwhelming feature of the executives' evaluations is that none of Carter's administrative techniques were considered successful in increasing presidential power. It is particularly devastating that reorganization and budgeting were among the most negatively evaluated given the priority assigned to them by Carter.

Analyzing the evaluations of reorganization and budgeting in greater detail demonstrates the failure of the Carter management

Table 6
Evaluations of the Effectiveness of Specific Administrative Techniques in the Carter Administration

Administrative Technique	Mean Response
Reorganization (impact on agency)	3.829
Reorganization (improvement in management)	3.173
SES (improvement in management)	3.550
SES (improvement in presidential control)	3.1994
Staffing (capacity for oversight)	3.756
Staffing (degree of actual oversight)	3.250
ZBB (management effectiveness)	3.776
ZBB (reordering budget priorities)	3.867

program. For example, the executives felt that the Carter reorganization efforts had little positive impact on their agencies and were only marginally successful in improving presidential management. These evaluations reinforce the conclusion reached in Chapter 4: although Carter heavily emphasized reorganization, his efforts had limited success.

In written comments accompanying the questionnaires, many executives stated that SES was difficult to evaluate because it was so new. However, with that caveat, the executives went on to suggest that SES was unlikely to improve management in the agencies, although by a slight margin they felt that the program would provide the president with greater control over career executives.

The executives also felt that the Carter White House staff did not exert much administrative oversight, which from the bureaucratic perspective was fine because they also felt the Carter staff did not have the capacity to successfully oversee the implementation of programs. The rejection of staffing as a management tool in the Carter administration may reflect the timing of the survey. Although Carter changed his staff system in July 1979 (moving away from cabinet government), that change may not have been reflected in the survey responses.

Zero base budgeting (ZBB) was the most negatively evaluated of all the management techniques (means of 3.776 and 3.867). This is a very telling evaluation, since the Carter administration stressed ZBB as a way of reordering budget priorities. The executives felt that ZBB was effective for neither presidential management nor reordering budget allocations. In fact, one executive referred to ZBB as a "joke" because of its ability to change the incremental nature of the budget process.

Comparing the evaluations of management in the Carter administration with the evaluations of presidential management in general provides even greater insight into the success of administrative techniques. Because each president emphasizes different techniques in his management program, it was expected that the Carter evaluations would differ somewhat from the general evaluations of presidential management. However, because each president can choose from only a limited number of management techniques and builds on the efforts of previous administrations (management as a historical trend), it was also expected that there should be similarities in the evaluations of administrative techniques. Table 7 compares presidential management in general and the Carter management program using the percentage of positive and negative evaluations as the basis for comparison.[7]

As expected, there are similarities that cut across presidential administrations. For example, in both evaluations reorganization is perceived as an ineffective tool for presidential management. On the other hand, personnel (here referring to the use of political and career executives) is seen as an effective tool for presidential management. This evaluation is further proof that career officials accept the manipulation of personnel—not in the negative sense of the Nixon administration, but rather in a positive sense of the president making use of political appointees.

There are also differences in the evaluations, indicating that bureaucrats believe it is possible for a president to place his mark on management through the techniques he chooses. Unfortunately, the Carter administration's mark seems to be primarily negative. For example, the bureaucrats generally evaluated staffing as an effective tool of presidential management, yet the Carter staffing efforts were evaluated much more negatively (a difference of 24 percent in the negative evaluation). This difference is not surprising, given that Carter was the first president since Harry S Truman to not use his

Table 7
Comparison of General Evaluations of Presidential Management and Management in the Carter Administration

Technique	Percent Positive Evaluation of Presidential Management	Percent Negative Evaluation of Presidential Management	Percent Positive Evaluation of Carter Management	Percent Negative Evaluation of Carter Management
Reorganization	31	42	41	59
Personnel	64	19	57	43
Staffing	44	32	44	56
Budgeting	65	18	32	68

staff to oversee policy implementation. Instead, Carter relied on cabinet government for most of the term. As a result, the bureaucrats regarded the Carter staff as ineffective in their management capabilities.

A comparison of the budgeting evaluations is even more startling. Budgeting in the Carter administration was perceived much more negatively than was budgeting in general. As suggested earlier, the difference may partially result from comparing a general evaluation of budgeting with a specific budgeting technique (ZBB). A particular technique (especially, it seems, ZBB) may create more enemies than presidential involvement in the budget process. The evaluation differences are so dramatic (65 percent positive for budgeting in general and 68 percent negative for budgeting in the Carter administration) that presidents might be better served to abandon budgeting technique and concentrate on flexing political muscle in the budget process. This approach is exactly that of the Reagan administration.

EVALUATING THE EFFECTIVENESS OF PRESIDENTIAL MANAGEMENT: THE REAGAN ADMINISTRATION

The administrative policies of the Reagan administration are an excellent contrast to those of the Carter administration because of the differences in their management styles. While the Carter administration placed its emphasis on administrative techniques, the Reagan administration has emphasized a more political strategy. Thus, there is the opportunity to evaluate and compare the effectiveness of two different models of presidential management. Given the established lack of success of the Carter model, the evaluation of the Reagan political model becomes even more important.

To confirm the importance of the Reagan management strategies established in Chapter 5 (a heavy emphasis on political appointees, budgeting, and to a lesser extent, deregulation), the 1984 survey asked administrative officials to evaluate their agencies' exposure to particular administrative techniques emphasized by the Reagan administration. Table 8 summarizes their responses.

This table reveals few surprises but clearly demonstrates the Carter and Reagan administrations' different approaches to management.

Presidential Power and Management Techniques

Table 8
Exposure to Management Techniques in the
Reagan Administration

Administrative Technique	Percent of Respondents Feeling Technique Used Frequently	Percent of Respondents Feeling Technique Used Infrequently
Reorganization	44	32
Staffing	36	42
Political appointees	71	16
SES	41	42
Budgeting	85	8
Deregulation	48	32

The bureaucrats identified the Reagan administration as placing a heavier emphasis on political appointees than did the Carter administration (71 percent indicating the Reagan administration's frequent reliance on political appointees versus 53 percent for the Carter administration). The Reagan administration was also noted as placing a heavy emphasis on budgeting (85 percent), as was the Carter administration (67 percent), but, as described in Chapter 5, a different type of budgeting. The bureaucrats also noted Reagan's emphasis on deregulation (48 percent), although their exposure to deregulation was not nearly as wide as to political appointees and budgeting. However, because deregulation would not affect all agencies equally, it is not surprising that the average exposure would be only moderate. The Reagan administration was also perceived as placing less emphasis on SES (41 percent), which is unusual given the widespread accusation of the administration's manipulation of SES. Reorganization is clearly less of a priority under Reagan (44 percent) than under Carter (53 percent), which again confirms the expected pattern. Finally, it is somewhat unexpected that the Reagan staff is not evaluated as an administrative tool used frequently (36 percent). With the exception of staffing, the evaluations contain few surprises but demonstrate the accuracy of the political model of management developed in Chapter 5.

However, an agency's level of exposure to an administrative technique only identifies how frequently the technique is being used, not its level of effectiveness. Therefore, the executives were asked to evaluate the effectiveness of specific administrative techniques. Table 9 summarizes their responses. The two most obvious results of the survey are the high levels of effectiveness of budgeting and political appointees. The evaluations of the Reagan budgeting approach (focusing on levels of funding rather than on budgeting technique) are the most impressive. Eighty-eight percent of the executives felt that the Reagan approach to budgeting has been effective in providing the president with greater control over policy implementation. Equally impressive, only 6 percent indicated that the

Table 9
Effectiveness of Management Techniques in the Reagan Administration

Administrative Technique	Percent of Respondents Feeling Technique Effective	Percent of Respondents Feeling Technique Ineffective
Reorganization	36	44
Staffing	40	29
Political appointees	64	19
SES	49	19
Budgeting	88	6
Deregulation	42	30

approach was generally ineffective. After comparing Reagan's positive evaluations on budgeting with the negative evalu ations of Carter's zero base budgeting, it seems that presidents should forget sophisticated budgeting techniques and concentrate on exercising presidential power in the budget process.

The Reagan administration's use of political appointees was also evaluated as an effective management technique (64 percent effective versus 19 percent ineffective). It is exactly the same percentage positive evaluation in Table 3, indicating that the administrators feel that the Reagan administration's heavy reliance on political appointees has expanded presidential power in an administrative area they feel appropriate.

The Senior Executive Service was evaluated as moderately effective (49 percent). This evaluation is very interesting, given the limited emphasis on SES indicated in Table 8. One of several possible explanations for this variance is that although few agencies have been exposed to manipulation of SES, that manipulation has been effective where it has been employed.

Interestingly, deregulation was evaluated as only moderately effective (42 percent effective, 30 percent ineffective). This evaluation appears to support the conclusion that although the Reagan administration has put considerable effort into developing a deregulation process, its ability to use the process to scale back the levels of federal regulatory policy has been limited. In fact, given the previous evaluations of budgeting and political appointees, success at deregulation may be determined more by their efforts to place "Reaganauts" in key regulatory positions and to cut the budgets of regulatory agencies than by Executive Order 12,291.

Last, as expected, both reorganization and staffing are not evaluated as particularly successful management techniques. The negative evaluation of reorganization (36 percent positive, 44 percent negative) continues the trend of negative evaluations of this management technique. However, in this case, it is not that large-scale reorganizations have not worked but rather that they have not been tried. Recognizing that reorganization had limited importance for the Reagan administration at the time of the survey, the respondents were asked whether they felt the administration had not used reorganization as a management tool and why. The survey options included: lack of interest on the part of the administration, lack of effectiveness of reorganization as a management tool, lack of reorganization authority, and lack of congressional cooperation. The responses are summarized in Table 10.

The most frequent response was the general lack of effectiveness of reorganization as a mangement tool (39 percent). However, although the administrators clearly feel that reorganizations are not effective (see the earlier evaluations), a significant percentage are not convinced that presidents have reached the same conclusion. Thirty-three percent feel the administration would have used large-scale reorganization (possibly eliminating the Departments of Education and Energy) and refrained only because of Congress's perceived lack of cooperation.

The Reagan administration's use of the White House staff (Table 9) was actually evaluated as slightly less effective (40 percent) than in the Carter administration (44 percent). However, this evaluation does not seem to reflect the bureaucrats' perception of the White House staff's capabilities. Seventy-eight percent of the officials evaluated the Reagan staff as either very capable, capable, or moderately capable; only 21 percent evaluated them as moderately incapable, incapable, or very incapable.[8] Perhaps this apparent discrepancy between capability and effectiveness reflects the lack of dispersion of power in the staff itself. During Reagan's first term, a small number of staff members (Deaver, Baker, Stockman, and Meese) seemed to dominate domestic policy. The other staff members may have been capable but not truly involved in the decision-making process.

Table 10
Reasons for the Nonuse of Reorganization in the Reagan Administration

Reason	Percent of Respondents
Lack of interest	27
Lack of effectiveness	39
Lack of authority	4
Lack of cooperation	33

Because of the obvious importance of political appointees, budgeting, and deregulation in Reagan's first term, follow-up questions were asked about each technique. For example, to better understand the evaluation of the Reagan administration's use of political appointees, the executives were asked to identify how well the Reagan appointees approximated the ideal role of political appointees and their effectiveness in shaping department or agency policies into agreement with the administration's overall goals.

Table 11 lists the executives' perceptions of the ideal and actual roles of political appointees. Again, administrative officials overwhelmingly support political appointees as strong advocates of presidential interests (88 percent) and offer very little support for political appointees as neutral administrators (6 percent) or advocates of agency interests (4 percent) or constituent interests (2 percent). Moreover, to a remarkable degree (88 percent), the officials surveyed felt the administration has been successful in placing strong supporters of the president in appointive positions. From the data, it appears that administrative officials and the president agree that the "proper" role of a political appointee is as a strong supporter of the president.

Table 11
Role of Political Appointees II

Role	Percent Response Ideal	Percent Response Actual
Advocate of president's interests	88	88
Neutral administrator	6	2
Advocate of agency's interests	4	2
Advocate of constituency's interests	2	8

The reason for the bureaucrats' response is evident in their later response about the reason for the Reagan administration's appointments. The choices provided included loyalty to the president, conservative ideology, political patronage, and experience as an administrator. Table 12 indicates that the officials feel the two most important reasons for the political appointments were loyalty to the president (40 percent) and ideology (34 percent). Equally interesting is the lack of support for patronage (12 percent) and experience (14 percent). In the eyes of the federal bureaucracy, Reagan has transformed an appointment process historically dominated by political patronage into one that now serves the president's interests.[9]

Finally, the respondents felt very strongly (85 percent) that the political appointees have been effective in helping to shape the department or agency's policies into agreement with the overall goals of the administration.[10] Richard Nixon and his aides may have worried about political appointees "going native" and adopting the agency or constituency perspective, but that is clearly not a concern for the Reagan administration.

Follow-up questions were also asked about the Reagan administration's budget policies. Having already assessed that the Reagan budget policies have increased presidential control, the administrators were questioned about the Reagan budget cut's effect on their agencies. The administrators were first asked whether the cuts had

Table 12
Reasons for the Appointment of Reagan Appointees

Criteria	Percent of Respondents
Loyalty	40
Ideology	34
Patronage	12
Experience	14

positively or negatively affected their department or agency's management capabilities. Sixty-seven percent felt that budget cuts had negatively affected their department or agency's management capabilities.[11] They were also asked to assess the degree to which the budget cuts have been successful in restructuring budget priorities. Seventy-three percent felt that they were.[12]

Clearly, although the administrators acknowledged the president's success in gaining control over the budget process, they also felt that the cuts have had an overall negative impact. Two implications are apparent in these responses. First, political power is not an infinite commodity, and a gain in budgetary power for the president quite naturally results in a loss of influence by departments and agencies. Second, increased presidential power in the budget process does not necessarily mean better administration. While administrative officials feel that Reagan has been successful in exerting greater control over the budget process, they also feel that power has been exerted in a manner that is detrimental to their agency interests.

Finally, because the Reagan administration has placed a high priority on deregulation, follow-up questions were asked about the impact of Executive Order 12,291. The executives were asked to assess deregulation's impact on presidential control of regulatory policy, the extent to which their department or agency has been affected by the regulatory changes, and the overall impact of Executive Order 12,291.

Sixty percent of the executives felt that the executive order increased the president's control over regulatory policy.[13] The respondents were more evenly divided about whether regulatory policy had become more cost-effective as a result of Executive Order 12,291. As indicated in Table 13, 44 percent of the respondents felt that regulatory policy had become more cost-effective. However, 36 percent felt there had been no change at all, and a surprising 20 percent felt that regulatory policy had actually become less cost-effective. For the overall impact of deregulation, 60 percent felt they had been moderately to very strongly affected, while 42 percent felt they had not been affected.[14] It is not surprising that the percentage answering positively is not higher, since Executive Order 12,291 is directed primarily at regulatory agencies and the sample includes

Table 13
Cost-Effectiveness of Deregulation in the Reagan Administration

Level of Cost-Effectiveness	Percent of Respondents
More cost-effective	44
No change in cost-effectiveness	36
Less cost-effective	20

many nonregulatory agencies. Finally, there was a moderate show of support for the overall impact of deregulation. Sixty percent of the officials rated the impact as between somewhat and very positive, and 40 percent rated the impact between somewhat and very negative.

Overall, then, the assessment of deregulation is mixed. While administrators feel that the general impact is slightly positive, they are not sure that regulatory policy has been made more cost-effective, which is one of the main concerns of Executive Order 12,291. Therefore, while the evaluation of deregulation is more positive than the evaluations of the management techniques used by the Carter administration, the political strategies used by the Reagan administration (political appointees and budgeting) are perceived as more successful than deregulation in increasing presidential power.

SUMMARY

In the evaluations of the Carter and Reagan management programs, the bureaucrats make a clear choice between competing administrative models. The Carter administration relied primarily on administrative techniques such as zero base budgeting and reorganization. By and large, the bureaucrats considered this approach (at least as applied by the Carter administration) to be very unsuccessful. The Reagan administration has made only limited use of administrative techniques and has concentrated on the exercise of political power through political appointees and budget cuts. The administrative officials considered this approach to be much more successful in increasing presidential power.

However, management programs represent only the external dimension of presidential power. A successful president must use both the external and internal dimensions of power.

NOTES

1. The domestic departments were the Department of Agriculture, Department of Commerce, Department of Energy, Department of Health and Human Services (Health, Education, and Welfare in the 1980 survey), Department of Housing and Urban Development, Department of the Interior, Department of Justice, Department of Labor, Department of the Treasury, Department of Transportation, Department of Education (1984), and Department of Energy (1984). The administrative agencies were Action, Civil Aeronautics Board, Commission on Civil Rights, Commodity Futures Trading Comission, Community Services Administration, Consumer Product Safety Commission, Environmental Protection Agency, Equal Employment Opportunity Commission, Federal Election Commission, Federal Home Loan Bank Board, Federal Labor Relations Authority, Federal Maritime Commission, Federal Mediation and Conciliation Service, Federal Reserve System, Federal Trade Commission, Merit System Protection Board, National Aeronautics and Space Administration, National Endowment for the Humanities, National Labor Relations Board, National Science Foundation, National Transportation Board, Nuclear Regulatory Commission, Office of Personnel Management, Postal Rate Commission, Securities and Exchange Commission, Small Business Administration, and Veterans Administration.

2. Since an acceptable response rate for mail questionnaires generally runs between 20 and 40 percent, it was felt that the 1980 response rate of 47 percent was excellent, and the 1984 response rate of 35 percent was quite good, especially given the politically sensitive nature of the questions. There was some evidence in written comments that federal officials are being inundated with questionnaires and have grown somewhat weary of filling them out, which may help explain the slightly diminished response rate in 1984.

3. Specific response rates are as follows.

Department	Percent of Response (1980)	Percent of Response (1984)
Agriculture	17	16
Commerce	11	10
Energy	9	10
Health, Education, and Welfare (Health and Human Services)	14	14
Housing and Urban Development	5	4
Interior	3	3
Justice	4	5
Labor	8	7
Treasury	5	3
Transportation	8	11
Education	0	5
Administrative	16	14
	102	102

Because of rounding, percentages will not always total 100.

4. Most evaluations used a 5-point scale, with an evaluation of 3 considered neutral. The neutral category is not presented; therefore, percentages will not total 100.

5. For example, a question such as "How do you feel the president's ability to manipulate the budget process rates as a management tool?" may get a very different answer from "How would you evaluate zero base budgeting as a management tool?"

6. Because the scale ranges only from 1 to 6, a difference of 1 may not seem significant in absolute terms; however, in terms of the scale, it is very significant.

7. Because no single question tapped this dimension, indexes based on Likert scales were created for each administrative technique, using the two previously cited questions concerning that technique.

8. Exact breakdowns are as follows: very capable (7 percent), capable (25 percent), moderately capable (46 percent), moderately incapable (14 percent), incapable (6 percent), very incapable (1 percent).

9. An obvious question concerns the lack of emphasis on experience. While loyalty and ideology may tie the political appointee to the president, does it make him a capable administrator? If not, what are the long-term implications for department and agency management?

10. Exact breakdowns are as follows: extremely effective (18 percent), very effective (32 percent), effective (35 percent), ineffective (9 percent), very ineffective (3 percent), extremely ineffective (2 percent).

11. Exact breakdowns are as follows: very positive impact (2 percent), positive impact (14 percent), somewhat positive impact (15 percent), somewhat negative impact (32 percent), negative impact (35 percent), very negative impact (10 percent).

12. Percent agreeing and disagreeing with the statement on increased structuring of budget priorities were as follows: strongly agree (25 percent), agree (48 percent), disagree (17 percent), strongly disagree (5 percent), no opinion (4 percent).

13. Exact breakdowns are as follows: great deal more control (22 percent), more control (38 percent), no more control (25 percent), less control (15 percent).

14. Exact breakdowns are as follows: very strongly affected (10 percent), strongly affected (20 percent), moderately affected (30 percent), somewhat unaffected (17 percent), very little affected (21 percent), not affected at all (4 percent).

7

The Limits of Management Techniques and the Importance of Presidential Leadership

THE INTERNAL DIMENSION OF PRESIDENTIAL POWER: PRESIDENTIAL LEADERSHIP SKILLS

The analysis of the executives' evaluations of presidential management in the Carter and Reagan administrations indicates that from a bureaucratic perspective, the presidents' management techniques and styles vary in their ability to improve presidential control over policy implementation. Specifically, it seems that the political model of presidential management used by the Reagan administration was much more successful than the administrative model used by Carter.

Earlier, it was suggested that administrative techniques are only a single dimension of presidential power (the external dimension). There is also an internal dimension of presidential power consisting of a variety of factors "internal" to the way a president organizes and carries out activities. Among these factors are the president's management style, personal characteristics, and political skills.

The internal and external dimensions of presidential power are interrelated, and both are important for the success of presidential management. Thus, there should be a strong correlation between the internal dimension of power and effective management, as well as between the internal and external dimensions of presidential power or between presidential skills and administrative techniques.

To investigate these relationships, both surveys asked the administrative executives to evaluate the importance of a series of personal characteristics and political skills for effective management.[1] To determine how Presidents Jimmy Carter and Ronald Reagan rank along this dimension of presidential power, the administrative executives were also asked to evaluate the degree to which the two presidents had these qualities. Tables 14 and 15 summarize the evaluations of personal characteristics for Carter and Reagan respectively. Tables 16 and 17 summarize the evaluations of the level of political skills in the two administrations.

The first column of Tables 14 and 15 indicates that the bureaucrats found the personal characteristics to be important for effective management. According to their evaluations, courage, intelligence, vision, and self-confidence are the personal characteristics most important for a president wishing to become an effective manager.

Flexibility and sincerity are also considered important, but to a lesser degree, while the importance of humor, vanity, and partisanship is evaluated quite low. Differences between the 1980 and 1984 surveys are negligible, with primarily positive changes and the most important changes occurring in humor, vanity, and partisanship, which are still generally not considered very important for presidential management.

Unfortunately for Carter, the third column in Table 14 suggests that the administrators found him to be relatively strong on only two of the most important characterstics (intelligence and self-confidence). They were evenly split in their perception of Carter's political courage and evaluated his sense of vision negatively (55 percent felt that Carter lacked a sense of vision versus 17 percent who felt he had it). Given the importance the administrators attached to vision (second most important character trait), this evaluation is particularly damning. Overall, the evaluations of Carter are generally low, even on those characteristics not evaluated as important for successful management.

Carter also suffers in comparison with the evaluations of Reagan in Table 15. Reagan's evaluations are much higher on five out of nine characteristics. On those characteristics considered most important for successful management, Reagan averages 23 percent higher. The difference in the bureaucratic evaluation of the level of self-confidence is a startling 46 percent. Among the most important characteristics, the only one in which Carter was evaluated more

Table 14
Personal Characteristics: 1980

Character Trait	Percent Feeling Trait Important for Management	Percent Feeling Trait Not Important for Management	Percent Finding Trait in President Carter	Percent Not Finding Trait in President Carter
Flexibility	77	8	39	32
Courage	84	6	37	37
Intelligence	83	4	47	24
Vision	84	7	17	55
Self-confidence	85	7	46	22
Sincerity	66	13	65	19
Humor	30	36	15	46
Vanity	21	44	38	29
Partisanship	50	23	38	30

Table 15
Personal Characteristics: 1984

Character Trait	Percent Feeling Trait Important for Management	Percent Feeling Trait Not Important for Management	Percent Finding Trait in President Reagan	Percent Not Finding Trait in President Reagan
Flexibility	78	7	30	41
Courage	87	1	70	9
Intelligence	86	1	32	39
Vision	93	2	45	20
Self-confidence	86	3	92	3
Sincerity	66	4	53	26
Humor	46	25	76	16
Vanity	35	41	44	35
Partisanship	56	13	21	56

positively than Reagan was intelligence. By 15 percent, the respondents felt that intelligence was more characteristic of Carter than Reagan. However, the edge in the evaluations of personal characteristics clearly belongs to Reagan. That personal skills are important for presidential management and that Reagan is evaluated so positively on them is a possible explanation as to why his management program has been evaluated so highly.

The data in Tables 16 and 17 indicate that many of the political skills that make up the internal dimension of presidential power are evaluated as even more important for management than are the personal characteristics. Respondents believe that ability to relate to Congress, skill in timing issues, ability to maintain public trust, ability to assess political realities, and ability to sell programs are particularly important for effective management (all of them evaluated as important by over 85 percent of the respondents in both surveys). Again, changes between the two surveys are small, with only one change (maintaining a positive image—for obvious reasons) increasing in importance by more than 10 percent in the 1984 survey.

Interestingly, in neither survey is the ability to relate to the bureaucracy considered one of the most important political skills (realizing, of course, that all of the skills are evaluated as important by at least 50 percent of the respondents). This may indicate that the bureaucrats have come to accept a degree of animosity between the president and the bureaucracy as a natural state of affairs, and that as long as the animosity does not get out of hand, it need not interfere with the effective management of programs.

The third and fourth columns of Table 16 indicate that the bureaucrats perceived Carter as having few of the political skills necessary for successful management. This was particularly true of Carter's ability to relate to the other institutions of government (59 percent found Carter unable to relate to Congress, while only 4 percent considered that he could relate to Congress; 76 percent found Carter unable to relate to the bureaucracy, versus 5 percent that found him able to do so). The respondents evaluated Carter moderately positive on only two skills: ability to relate to his staff and ability to relate to the press. Even here, the percentages are less than overwhelming (54 percent for staff and 32 percent for the press).

Table 16
Political Skills: 1980

Skill	Percent Finding Skill Important for Management	Percent Finding Skill Not Important for Management	Percent Finding Skill in President Carter	Percent Not Finding Skill in President Carter
Ability to relate to Congress	96	3	4	59
Ability to relate to staff	80	4	54	12
Ability to assess political realities	95	3	24	33
Ability to relate to interest groups	62	5	25	25
Ability to relate to press	72	3	32	20
Ability to relate to bureaucracy	69	6	5	76
Skill in timing issues	85	4	15	47
Organizational skills	53	16	15	48
Ability to maintain public trust	94	3	28	40
Ability to avoid isolation	74	5	30	30
Ability to maintain image	67	12	20	42
Skill in shifting positions	65	12	15	39
Ability to sell programs	87	4	7	57

Table 17
Political Skills: 1984

Skill	Percent Finding Skill Important for Management	Percent Finding Skill Not Important for Management	Percent Finding Skill in President Reagan	Percent Not Finding Skill in President Reagan
Ability to relate to Congress	94	1	43	27
Ability to relate to staff	80	4	64	15
Ability to assess political realities	94	2	57	18
Ability to relate to interest groups	56	11	50	16
Ability to relate to press	71	6	64	18
Ability to relate to bureaucracy	66	8	9	70
Skill in timing issues	86	12	50	18
Organizational skills	51	19	24	44
Ability to maintain public trust	93	3	75	11
Ability to avoid isolation	76	2	43	30
Ability to maintain image	79	8	89	4
Skill in shifting positions	59	9	56	20
Ability to sell programs	86	6	72	10

The negative evaluations of Carter's personal and political skills clearly represent a failure of Carter's "outsiders" approach to politics. By his own words (especially during his 1976 campaign for the presidency), Carter portrayed himself as a political outsider, as one aloof from the "mess" in Washington. It may well be that the virtue of being a political outsider during the campaign turned into a vice in attempting to govern. The bureaucratic officials' evaluations indicate that Carter did not seem to have the political skills necessary for effective presidential management (on nine of the political skills, 25 percent or less of the respondents found the skill in Carter).

A consideration of the level of political skill found in Reagan reveals a very different picture. Table 17 (columns 3 and 4) demonstrates that the administrative officials evaluated Reagan as having a much higher level of political skill than Carter—especially on those skills identified as most important for successful presidential management. The average of respondents finding these skills in Reagan is an incredible 44 percentage points higher than Carter (a startling 65 percent higher for ability to sell programs and 47 percent higher for ability to maintain the public trust).

Reagan's weakest evaluation is of his ability to relate to the bureaucracy, which given the positive evaluations of Reagan's management program reinforces the observation that this political skill generally may be overrated. On almost every other skill, Reagan is evaluated very positively. Thus, it would seem a president can have a successful management program without an innate ability to relate to the bureaucracy.

OTHER LIMITS ON PRESIDENTIAL MANAGEMENT

This analysis confirms a strong relationship between the internal dimension of power and presidential management. It is also possible that bureaucratic perceptions of the motives behind the president's management program might explain the success or failure of a particular administrative technique. The bureaucracy may perceive a management program as the administration's legitimate attempt to gain control over policy implementation. If so, the bureaucracy would likely accept the program's validity, and the technique involved would be successful in increasing presidential control over policy implementation. It is also possible that the bureaucracy would not accept the administrative technique's perceived motivations or purposes (evidence suggests that the Nixon management initiatives were regarded in this manner).[2] The bureaucracy may also see the program as an exercise in futility: as the needless production of paperwork that will never even be read (evidence also suggests that the planned program budgeting system was perceived in this fashion).[3] If this is correct, then there should be a strong correlation between legitimacy and the evaluations of the specific management techniques used in the Carter and Reagan administrations.

To test this relationship, the administrative executives were asked a variety of questions concerning their perception of the legitimacy of presidential management. Two questions were directed at the motives behind presidential management and two at the impact of presidential management. The results are summarized in Table 18.

As the data suggest, the bureaucrats are somewhat skeptical of the legitimacy of presidential management. In the 1980 Carter administration survey, 64 percent felt that the primary motive of the programs was to increase presidential power at the expense of the bureaucracy. Only slightly more than half of the respondents (56 percent) felt that the programs were designed to provide more responsible government. When queried about the impact of presidential management, bureaucratic skepticism was even more evident.

Table 18
Legitimacy of Presidential Management

Motive or Impact	Percent Agree Carter	Percent Disagree Carter	Percent Agree Reagan	Percent Disagree Reagan
More responsible government	56	44	58	42
Increase presidential power at the expense of bureaucracy	64	36	60	40
Busywork	77	23	55	45
Symbolic	52	48	48	52

A clear majority (77 percent) felt that the major impact of the Carter management program was to create busywork—wasting the bureaucrats' time in fruitless endeavors.

The data on the Reagan administration present a picture that is much less clear. Only 60 percent of the respondents felt that the Reagan management program's primary motive is to increase presidential power at the expense of the bureaucracy—a bare 2 percent less felt that the primary motive is more responsible government. Only 55 percent felt that the Reagan management programs are a waste of time. While there is a measure of support for the symbolic importance of management in both the Carter (52 percent) and Reagan (48 percent) administrations, as many bureaucrats rejected the possibility as accepted it. Overall, the responses indicate that the management program's perceived legitimacy may be important in explaining the evaluations of specific administrative techniques, although it is expected to be more important for the evaluations of the Carter management program than for the Reagan program.

There may also be a structural explanation for the variance in the evaluations of the Carter and Reagan administrative techniques. For example, evaluations may vary according to the type of policy involved with the specific agencies. Randall B. Ripley and Grace A. Franklin, using a modification of Theodore J. Lowi's classification of policy types, suggest that there are differing structural patterns of influence among the Congress, the bureaucracy, and the president, according to the types of policy under consideration.[4] According to Ripley and Franklin, the primary decisionmaker changes with the type of policy involved. For instance, in distributive policy and regulatory policy, there is a congressional/bureaucratic dominance in decision making. The president is the dominant decisionmaker only in redistributive policy. It is likely, therefore, that administrative techniques that attempt to extend presidential power into areas not already under presidential influence (distributive policy and regulatory policy) will be perceived negatively by the bureaucrats affected, that is, as threatening to disrupt existing relationships (triple alliances) that control policy-making in these areas. To determine whether there is a relationship between policy types and bureaucratic evaluations of administrative techniques, the agencies involved in the surveys were classified according to policy type.[5]

In the 1980 survey of the Carter administration, the response sample shows an overrepresentation of administrative agencies (45 percent). This is possibly the result of the survey structure, which was designed to include primarily administrative personnel. The responses for other policy types are as follows: distributive policy, 19 percent; regulatory policy, 18 percent; and redistributive policy, 7 percent.

The response sample for the Reagan administration is more representative. In this case, administrative agencies made up 35 percent of the response sample, with 31 percent for distributive policy, 22 percent for redistributive policy, and 13 percent for regulatory policy. To test the relationship, policy types and bureaucratic evaluations of presidential management were also correlated.

THE IMPORTANCE OF LEADERSHIP SKILLS

The hypothesized relationships between the evalutions of the administrative techniques used in the Carter administration (reorganization, the Senior Executive Service [SES], staffing, and zero base budgeting [ZBB]) and the Reagan administration (reorganization, budgeting, deregulation, and political appointees) and explanatory variables (presidential skills, legitimacy, and policy types) were investigated through the use of cross-tabulation analysis.[6] The results for the Carter administration are presented in Table 19.

The results for the Carter administration confirm many of the expected relationships: skills, policy type, and legitimacy all form significant correlations with at least one of the administrative techniques. The data also indicate an interesting pattern to the correlations. The structural variable–policy type forms a strong, statistically significant relationship with reorganization. Presidential skills and legitimacy correlate with the rest of the administrative techniques. Thus, there are two possible explanations for the negative evaluations of the Carter management program.

The strong relationship between policy type and reorganization would at first glance seem to support the hypothesis that reorganization would be the only management technique that threatens agency external relationships, and therefore negative evaluations would be the most prevalent in agencies involved in distributive policy. However, a close examination of the frequency distributions in the cross-tabulation analysis presented in Table 20 indicates that

Table 19

Summary Statistics: Limitations of Presidential Management (Carter)

Relationship	Chi^2	Degrees of Freedom	Significance	Measures of Association
Reorganization by skills	0.03640	1	0.8487	phi = 0.02413
Reorganization by policy type	10.65260	4	0.0308	Cramer's V = 0.22964
Reorganization by legitimacy	0.02189	1	0.8824	phi = 0.01978
SES by skills	8.07376	1	0.0045	phi = 0.20607
SES by policy type	5.08081	4	0.2791	Cramer's V = 0.15860
SES by legitimacy	6.70155	1	0.0096	phi = 0.18732
Staffing by skills	9.19505	1	0.0024	phi = 0.18732
Staffing by policy type	1.37427	4	0.8427	Cramer's V = 0.15860
Staffing by legitimacy	0.03939	1	0.8427	phi = 0.02314
ZBB by skills	22.92934	1	0.0000	phi = 0.3407
ZBB by policy type	1.42535	4	0.8398	Cramer's V = 0.08400
ZBB by legitimacy	8.86052	1	0.0029	phi = 0.21455

Table 20
Reorganization by Policy Type

Total and Percentage

	Admin.	Distrib.	Regulatory	Redistrib.	None of the Above
Positive evaluation	44 41.8%	21 10.4%	10 5.0%	4 2.0%	6 3.0%
Negative evaluation	47 23.3%	17 8.4%	27 13.4%	11 5.4%	15 7.4%
Neutral evaluation	91 45.0%	38 18.8%	37 18.3%	15 7.4%	21 10.4%

chi^2 = 10.65260

Cramer's V = 0.22964

the relationship may not be as straightforward as first expected. For example, in agencies involved with distributive policy, positive evaluations of reorganization actually outnumbered negative evaluations (21 to 17). Instead, it is in the agencies involved with regulatory and redistributive policies that reorganization is evaluated most negatively. Therefore, alternative explanations are needed.

The first assumption—that agencies dominated by subgovernment politics would be most "threatened" by reorganization and thus most likely to provide negative evaluations—is clearly incorrect. Although the data do not really allow for full consideration of this issue, it would seem that these agencies, because of their subgovernment relationships, are best able to resist or even defeat reorganizations that would disrupt the subgovernment. Thus, they have little to fear from presidential reorganizations since the most threatening reorganizations never reach the agencies.

Conversely, agencies involved with redistributive policy are likely to have more tenuous relationships with clientele groups (who are also much less powerful) and are thus likely to have less support in Congress. Therefore, they would be less likely to be able to resist the intrusion of presidential reorganizations, which could explain the negative evaluations.

Finally, that regulatory agencies also evaluate reorganization negatively may be explained by their institutional separation from the rest of the executive branch, which ordinarily shields them from the type of intrusion in agency affairs represented by presidential reorganizations. Again, none of these suggested explanations can be proven or disproven by the data. However, it is clear that the evaluations of reorganization do vary across policy types in directions not originally assumed, thus pointing out the need for further research in this area.

The absence of significant relationships between policy type and staffing, SES, and budgeting is also of interest. The cross-tabulations indicate that policy type does not explain the negative evaluations of these administrative techniques. This absence of a relationship is undoubtedly related to the idea that these administrative techniques may change the internal operating functions of the agencies, but not their external relations. Therefore, it is not surprising that the structural variable and the remaining administrative techniques are not highly correlated.

That both presidential skills and legitimacy are strongly correlated with the remaining administrative techniques suggests that a particular president can use his political skills to affect the bureaucratic perception of his management program, thus possibly increasing presidential management. Take, for example, budgeting. Bureaucrats seem to have a positive perception of budgeting as a general tool of presidential management. However, zero base budgeting in the Carter administration was perceived quite negatively. Given the negative evaluation of Carter on the external dimension of presidential power and the subsequent strong correlation between budgeting and skills, it seems that Carter's lack of skills was the major reason for zero base budgeting's negative evaluation. Carter was not able to use his skills to gain control of the budget process by convincing the bureaucrats of the validity of zero base budgeting as a management tool because in bureaucratic eyes he did not have those skills. This is particularly evident given the strong correlation between legitimacy and zero base budgeting. Zero base budgeting did not succeed at least partially because career bureaucrats were not convinced it was a legitimate tool of presidential management.

Table 21 summarizes the correlations between important administrative techniques used in the Reagan administration and the evaluations of presidential skills, policy type, and legitimacy. The most important finding is the strong correlations between presidential skills and political appointees and budgeting. It seems that the positive evaluations of the level of presidential skills are associated with the use of political appointees and the exercise of presidential power in the budgeting process. This is not unexpected given the political model of administration exercised in the Reagan administration. Certainly, the use of presidential power in the administrative process would depend on a modicum of political skill—skills that the respondents obviously felt that Reagan has in abundance. These are, in fact, the very skills that the bureaucrats identified as important for presidential management. Reagan has also been helped in gaining acceptance of his management program (relying heavily on political appointees and budgeting) by the fact that there is a high level of acceptance of these techniques as presidential management tools. When this latent acceptance of political appointees and budgeting is combined with Reagan's high level of political skill, it is clear why he has been remarkably successful in gaining acceptance of his management programs. Thus, it would seem that a high level of political skill may be an important determinant of the success of a president's management program.

It is also interesting that for reorganization and deregulation, there is no significant relationship with either presidential skills or policy type. The explanation with regard to reorganization may be in the relative absence of large-scale reorganizations in the Reagan administration. Those reorganizations that have taken place have been much smaller in scope and confined to specific agencies. Obviously, such reorganizations will not create the type of disruptions inherent in cabinet-level reorganizations. Therefore, it is unlikely that a president will need to use his skills to "sell" this type of program. What would have been extremely meaningful would have been an effort by Reagan to create a large-scale reorganization similar to those under Carter. Given the federal bureaucracy's resistance to reorganizations, it would be interesting to see whether Reagan could use his considerable political skills to carry out a large-scale reorganization plan. For example, would Reagan have been able to sell Congress and the federal bureaucracy a reorganization plan to eliminate the Department of Energy?

There is also no significant relationship between deregulation and

Table 21
Summary Statistics: Limitations of Presidential Management (Reagan)

Relationship	Chi^2	Degrees of Freedom	Significance	Measures of Association
Reorganization by skills	3.96267	8	0.6050	Cramer's V = 0.12160
Reorganization by policy type	14.28843	12	0.2827	Cramer's V = 0.09897
Reorganization by legitimacy	1.34201	4	0.8542	Cramer's V = 0.09897
Budgeting by skills	31.26833	10	0.0005	Cramer's V = 0.34157
Budgeting by policy type	16.21740	15	0.3678	Cramer's V = 0.19792
Budgeting by legitimacy	6.18809	5	0.2293	Cramer's V = 0.22967
Deregulation by skills	12.97088	10	0.2253	Cramer's V = 0.22422
Deregulation by policy type	21.20523	15	0.1304	Cramer's V = 0.22967
Deregulation by legitimacy	5.74826	5	0.3315	Cramer's V = 0.20712
Appointees by skills	28.92934	10	0.0014	Cramer's V = 0.32874
Appointees by policy type	11.78817	15	0.6950	Cramer's V = 0.16874
Appointees by legitimacy	11.77837	5	0.0386	Cramer's V = 0.29379

policy type. It was thought that because deregulation was directed primarily at agencies involved in regulatory policy, their program evaluations would differ greatly from the other agencies in the study, and a significant relationship would be found between the evaluations of deregulation and policy type. However, the data indicate that this is not the case. There are two possible explanations for this lack of relationship. First, the number of regulatory agencies in the sample is very small (only 13 percent of the responses), and it may be that the cross-section of regulatory agencies that was surveyed was not large enough to form a statistically significant relationship. However, a second, more likely explanation relates to the evaluations of the deregulation program. The overall evaluations were mostly middle range—neither strongly positive nor negative. It was hypothesized that a significant finding concerning the regulatory agencies might be buried in the data. The findings indicated by the correlations in Table 21 indicate that this is probably not the case. It might be that the critics of deregulation are correct—the administration has not devoted enough time or resources to the program to create a significant impact even within the regulatory agencies. Thus, if deregulation is to take place, it seems more likely to come through the use of political appointees or through budgeting, not Executive Order 12,291. There is little evidence in the survey that regulatory relief has significantly affected the regulatory processes of the federal bureaucracy.

SUMMARY

In this review of the survey results, the importance of leadership for successful presidential management of the policy process has become evident. Examining the correlations between the bureaucratic evaluations of specific administrative techniques applied in the Carter and Reagan administrations and the evaluations of presidential skills has demonstrated an important explanation for the varying degrees of success of the Carter and Reagan management programs.

The administrative model employed by the Carter administration floundered at least partially because of a perceived lack of leadership on Carter's part. This is especially true with regard to one of the key features of the Carter management program—zero base budgeting (ZBB). The data on ZBB suggest that one of the reasons for its lack of success was Carter's inability to mobilize the political skill necessary to convince career bureaucrats of the legitimacy of the program. Thus, presidential management suffered for the absence of political skill.

The political model of management adopted by President Reagan has been successful for two reasons. First, the administration chose to emphasize a management program that relies on techniques (political appointees and manipulating the budget process) that have a high level of acceptance within the federal bureaucracy. Second, the political model chosen by the administration demands a high level of political skill that the bureaucratic evaluations indicate Reagan has almost to excess. Thus, given the high priority bureaucrats attach to political skill, for successful management, presidential leadership's importance in the success of the Reagan management program is clear.

Structural explanations can also be found for the lack of success of specific management techniques. While further research is needed to pinpoint the exact nature of the relationship, it is evident that the type of policy with which an agency is concerned is related to the perceived success of reorganization efforts. The relative importance of leadership and structure for presidential management remains to be determined. The Carter administration used reorganization to challenge existing bureaucratic relationships but for a variety of reasons (among which was the lack of political skill) was unsuccessful. The Reagan administration seems to have the skill necessary to carry out large-scale reorganizations but has not attempted to do so. Thus, for now, the relative importance of leadership and structure cannot be determined.

NOTES

1. The specific personal characteristics and political skills used in the survey were taken from Ross Clayton and William Lammers, "Presidential Leadership Reconsidered: Contemporary View of Top Federal Officials," *Presidential Studies Quarterly*, vol. 8 (Winter 1978), pp. 237–244.

2. Joel Havemann, "OMB's 'Management by Objective' Produces Goals of Uneven Quality," *National Journal*, vol. 5 (August 18, 1973), pp. 1201–1210.

3. Allen Schick, "A Death in the Bureaucracy: The Demise of Federal PPB," *Public Administration Review*, vol. 29 (1969).

4. For more information on the importance of policy type, see Randall B. Ripley and Grace A. Franklin, *Congress, the Bureaucracy, and Public Policy* (Homewood, Ill.: Dorsey Press, 1976) and Theodore J. Lowi, "Four Systems of Policy, Politics and Choice," *Public Administration Review*, vol. 32 (1972).

5. To the types suggested by Ripley and Franklin, an additional type—administrative policy—has been added primarily because of the emphasis on administrative executives.

6. Even though this survey does not constitute a true random sample (the emphasis on position precluded true randomness), tests of significance will still be employed because of the pioneering nature of the research. Therefore, as noted by Robert A. Bernstein and James A. Dyer, *An Introduction to Political Science Methods* (Englewood Cliffs, N.J.: Prentice-Hall, 1979), pp. 162–163, "if the apparent association is not strong enough to be statistically significant for a random sample, it is reason enough to ignore the association. If the association is found to be statistically significant, we cannot be as confident as with a random sample that it would hold for the theoretical population. Thus the test serves as a veto in the case of nonrandom sample, but it is less powerful as a reason to accept the conclusion than in the case of the random sample."

Conclusion: The Future of Presidential Management

Presidential management is based on the two dimensions of presidential power. The external dimension of power consists of presidential actions; that is, programs designed to give the president greater control over policy implementation. These actions are based on administrative techniques such as reorganization, the manipulation of personnel, staffing, and budgeting. However, the external dimension of power by itself does not necessarily guarantee the president greater control over implementation of his programs. Rather, implementation also requires the internal dimension of power: the personal and political skills that a president brings with him when he assumes office. Together, the external and internal dimensions of power may provide the president with the means to ensure successful policy implementation; alone, neither will be successful.

THE EXTERNAL DIMENSION OF POWER

The 1930s saw not only massive social, economic, and political upheavals in the capitalist world but also the emergence of a larger role for the federal government in previously "private" sectors of American life. With the federal government's growth in responsibility came a concurrent growth in the size and complexity of the executive departments. However, as the executive departments grew, presidents expressed increasing dissatisfaction with their ability to ensure that their legislative programs were not modified beyond recognition during the implementation process. The bureaucracy has not been overly impressed with presidential influence and has various "escape routes" from presidential control. Presidents, in turn, have lacked the constitutional and institutional authority to control the bureaucracy. Consequently, presidents have sought new techniques for increasing their power to control the bureaucracy, and thus policy implementation.

At the same time, public administrationists began to develop a variety of administrative techniques, stressing the principles of hierarchy and control of personnel and information that would ensure executive control of large-scale public organizations. From the beginning, it was a marriage of convenience. Presidents wanted to increase their power to control policy implementation, and public administrationists wanted the chance to apply their techniques in the real world. In President Franklin D. Roosevelt's administration, the President's Commission on Administrative Management consummated the marriage when public administrationists successfully lobbied for the introduction of reorganization and staffing into the federal government.

Since Franklin Roosevelt's administration, all modern presidents have sought to increase presidential power in order to increase their ability to control policy implementation. Each president has adopted a particular management style, consisting of his orientation to management (what he perceives to be important management problems and how management techniques can be applied to solve these problems) and a mixture of administrative tools (such as reorganization, the manipulation of personnel, staffing, and budgeting).

This empirical investigation of presidential management suggests that the federal bureaucracy has at least partially accepted the president's role as manager. The positive evaluations of staffing, political appointees, and budgeting demonstrate presidential success in gaining bureaucratic acceptance of the use of the external dimension of power to improve presidential management.

However, there is still considerable resistance to reorganization as a tool of presidential management because, inter alia, it threatens the structural relationships that agencies have built with congressional committee elites and interest group elites. Reorganizations (when successful from a presidential perspective) increase presidential power at the expense of bureaucratic influence, resulting in bureaucratic opposition. Moreover, the analysis of presidential management suggests that presidents have been unable to impose reorganization on reluctant bureaucracies. The reorganization efforts of Presidents Richard M. Nixon and Jimmy Carter are recent examples of presidents unable to extend control over policy implementation through reorganization because of the opposition of an unwilling and unyielding bureaucracy. Therefore, although staffing, personnel, and budgeting may serve to increase presidential power and thus presidential management, reorganization clearly does not.

THE INTERNAL DIMENSION OF POWER

The successful application of administrative techniques depends on the use of presidential skills (the internal dimension of power). A president who wants to be a successful manager must be able to use both his political skills and administrative techniques.

The empirical investigation of the relationship between the internal dimension of power and presidential management suggests that bureaucrats find a number of personal characteristics (courage, intelligence, vision, and self-confidence) and political skills (ability to relate to Congress, ability to assess political realities, skill in timing issues, the ability to maintain public trust, and the ability to sell programs) important for effective presidential management. The extent to which a president has these skills and is able to use them effectively may determine the success of his management program.

The management programs of Presidents Jimmy Carter and Ronald Reagan serve as examples. There can be little doubt that Carter attempted to increase presidential power by using administrative techniques to control policy implementation. However, his success was minimal. Many of his reorganization plans were never implemented; his White House staff was considered ineffective in overseeing policy implementation; the Senior Executive Service has been evaluated negatively by academics, journalists, and most importantly by those participating in the program; and his chief budgeting initiative—zero base budgeting—was judged a failure in reordering budget priorities by those who used it. Given the strong correlation between the internal dimension of power and successful management, and the negative evaluations of Carter's political skills, one of the primary reasons for the Carter management programs' lack of success would seem to be his lack of leadership skills. Carter was unable to convince the bureaucracy of the legitimacy of his management programs because he lacked the political skills to do so. This fact was not lost on the bureaucracy. One administrative executive, in a note that accompanied the evaluation, said:

This administration has done its best to destroy the competitive civil service system in an attempt to find a convenient scapegoat for this country's problems. The president surrounded himself with people from Georgia who had no experience at the federal level. Their perception of the total system and their actions have created serious problems. Their inability or unwillingness to relate to Congress and the bureaucracy is a good example.

Another executive suggested that "there hasn't been a president who has understood how to manage the bureaucracy since Lyndon Johnson." Each of the respondents confirms that successful management involves the use of both the internal and external dimensions of presidential power—skills as well as administrative techniques.

In many ways, Ronald Reagan's management style is the opposite of Jimmy Carter's style—long on political skill, but short on management techniques. Clearly, the respondents felt that Reagan possesses greater leadership skills than Carter and has been better able to use them to gain control over policy implementation.

However, the limitations of the Reagan management style, while not as severe as those of Carter, still bear examination. The Reagan management style is highly personal, relying heavily on the president's leadership skills and a cadre of staff and political appointees intensely loyal to Ronald Reagan. The reliance on leadership skills to increase presidential control over policy implementation can become problematic if presidential leadership starts to fade as a result of situational changes or poor decisions. Successful leadership does not depend entirely on political and personal skills. It also depends on the historical moment, the political environment, and sometimes just plain luck. If Reagan were to lose his aura of leadership, managerial capability would soon follow.

Reagan's reliance on staff and political appointees also creates the danger of overzealousness. As demonstrated in the Nixon administration, the pursuit of presidential control can breed arrogance in a staff deeply committed to the program of a very popular president. The best protection against this danger is a president/manager who exercises a great deal of oversight. However, if Reagan has demonstrated one weakness as a manager, it has been his tendency to overdelegate. During the first term, this weakness was in part compensated for by a chief of staff and a White House inner circle that, through long service to the president, had become deeply attuned to his needs and weaknesses. By the second term, most of these staff members had either left government or had taken cabinet positions. The president has been left with a politically inexperienced staff, and, as a result, the weaknesses of his managerial style may become more important.

Reagan has been able to use his leadership skills to gain control of the levers of power in the executive branch in order to enact his conservative agenda. He has not, however, been able to enact the structural and procedural reforms that would institutionalize presidential control over the administrative process. Once Reagan and his considerable collection of political skills and leadership qualities have left office, will less skilled and talented presidents be able to maintain the presidential influence Reagan has obtained? History suggests this to be unlikely. A more realistic scenario would be for future presidents to either adopt the Reagan model or fail miserably because they lack presidential skill or to fall back on management techniques that seem to have dubious levels of success in the absence of presidential power.

The central problem is whether it is possible to institutionalize presidential management. One method by which this might occur is for a president of considerable leadership skills to propose and enact a series of management initiatives to bring policy implementation more directly under presidential control. It is also possible that the president's institutional authority for administration might be strengthened through constitutional amendment or a congressional action, thus giving all presidents a stronger administrative hand to play and perhaps diminishing the importance of presidential leadership.

Unfortunately, both occurrences seem unlikely in the near future. Therefore, the prognosis for successful presidential management is not positive. Most presidents will continue to muddle through. The very few that combine leadership skills with innovative management programs will be successful.

Bibliography

Aberbach, Joel D., and Rockman, Bert A. "Clashing Beliefs Within the Executive Branch," *American Political Science Review*, vol. 70 (June 1976).

Anderson, Patrick. *The President's Men* (New York: Doubleday, 1968).

Arterton, F. Christopher. "The Impact of Watergate on Children's Attitudes Toward Political Authority," *Political Science Quarterly*, vol. 89 (1974).

Barber, James David. *Presidential Character* (Englewood Cliffs, N.J.: Prentice-Hall, 1976).

Beam, David R. "Public Administration is Alive and Well in the White House," *Public Administration Review*, vol. 38 (1978).

Benze, James G., Jr. "Presidential Management: The View from the Bureaucracy," *Presidential Studies Quarterly*, vol. 15 (Fall 1986).

Benze, James G., Jr. "Presidential Reorganization as a Tactical Weapon," *Presidential Studies Quarterly*, vol. 15 (Winter 1986).

Bernstein, Robert A., and Dyer, James A. *An Introduction to Political Science Methods* (Englewood Cliffs, N.J.: Prentice-Hall, 1979).

Blalock, Hubert M., Jr. *Social Statistics* (New York: McGraw-Hill, 1972).

Blaumber, Herbert H.; Fuller, Carolyn; and Hare, H. Paul. "Response Rates in Postal Surveys," *Public Opinion Quarterly*, vol. 36 (Spring 1974).

Bonafede, Dom. "Carter Sounds Retreat from Cabinet Government," *National Journal Reprint Series* (November 18, 1978).

Bonafede, Dom. "White House Reorganization—Separating Smoke from Substance," *National Journal*, vol. 9 (August 20, 1977).

Burns, James MacGregor. *Presidential Government* (Boston: Houghton Mifflin Company, 1973).

Caputo, David A., and Cole, Richard L. "Presidential Control of the Senior Civil Service: Assessing the Strategies of the Nixon Years," *American Political Science Review*, vol. 73 (June 1979).

Clark, Timothy B. "Do the Benefits Justify the Costs? Prove It, Says the Administration," *National Journal*, vol. 13 (August 1, 1981).

Clayton, Ross, and Lammers, William. "Presidential Leadership Reconsidered: Contemporary View of Top Federal Officials," *Presidential Studies Quarterly*, vol. 8 (Winter 1978).

Conlin, Paul K. *FDR and the Origins of the Welfare State* (New York: Thomas Y. Crowell, 1967).

Cooper, Ann. "Congress Approves Civil Service Reforms," *Congressional Quarterly Weekly Report* (October 14, 1973).

Cooper, Ann. "Reagan Has Tamed the Regulatory Beast but Not Permanently Broken Its Grip," *National Journal*, vol. 17 (December 1, 1984).

Corrigan, Richard. "Congress Takes a Chip Off Carter's Energy Block," *National Journal*, vol. 9 (June 11, 1977).

Corwin, Edward S. *The President: Office and Powers*, 4th ed. (New York: New York University Press, 1957).

Cronin, Thomas E. *The State of the Presidency* (Boston: Little, Brown, 1975).

Demkovich, Linda E. "Team Player Schweiker May Be Paying a High Price for His Loyalty to Reagan," *National Journal*, vol. 15 (May 15, 1982).

Fallows, James. "The Passionless Presidency," *The Atlantic*, vol. 244 (May 1979).

Fallows, James. "The Passionless Presidency, Part II," *The Atlantic* (June 1979).

Finer, Herman. "The Hoover Commission Reports," *Political Science Quarterly*, vol. 64 (1949).

Fischer, Louis. *Presidential Spending Power* (Princeton, N.J.: Princeton University Press, 1975).

Florestano, Patricia. "The Characteristics of White House Staff Appointees from Truman to Nixon," *Presidential Studies Quarterly*, vol. 11 (Fall 1979).

Fullington, Michael Gregory. "Presidential Management and Executive Scandal," *Presidential Studies Quarterly*, vol. 10 (Winter 1979).

Gilmour, Robert S. "Controlling Regulation in the Reagan Administration: The Emergence of Central Clearance," paper presented at the Annual Conference of the New England Political Science Association, U.S. Naval War College, Newport, R.I. (April 13, 1984).

Goodnow, Frank. *Politics and Administration* (New York: Macmillan, 1900).

Gorham, William. "PPBS: Its Scope and Limits," *The Public Interest*, vol. 8 (Summer 1967).

Graham, Otis L. *Toward a Planned Society* (New York: Oxford University Press, 1976).

Gulick, Luther. *Papers on the Science of Administration* (New York: Institute of Public Administration, 1937).

Hale, Myron Q. "Presidential Influence, Authority, and Power and Economic Policy," in *Toward a Humanistic Science of Politics: Essays in Honor of Francis Dunham Woarmuth*, Dalmas H. Nelson and Richard L. Sklar, eds. (New York: University Press of America, 1983).

Hamilton, Alexander; Madison, James; and Jay, John. *The Federalist Papers* (New York: New American Library, 1961).

Hargrove, Erwin C. *The Power of the Modern Presidency* (New York: Alfred A. Knopf, 1974).

Havemann, Joel. "Carter's Reorganization Plans—Scrambling for Turf," *National Journal*, vol. 10 (May 20, 1978).

Havemann, Joel. "OMB's 'Management by Objective' Produces Goals of Uneven Quality," *National Journal*, vol. 5 (August 18, 1973).

Havemann, Joel. "Taking Up the Tools to Tame the Bureaucracy: Zero Base Budgeting and Sunset Legislation," *National Journal Reprint Series* (November 18, 1978).

Heclo, Hugh. *A Government of Strangers* (Washington, D.C.: The Brookings Institution, 1977).

Henry, Nicholas. *Public Administration and Public Affairs* (Englewood Cliffs, N.J.: Prentice-Hall, 1975).

Karl, Barry Dean. *Executive Reorganization and Reform in the New Deal* (Cambridge: Harvard University Press, 1963).

Karl, Barry Dean. "Public Administration and American History," *Public Administration Review*, vol. 36 (1976).

Kirschten, Dick. "Administration Using Carter-Era Reform to Manipulate the Levers of Government," *National Journal*, vol. 15 (April 19, 1983).

Kirschten, Dick. "Once Again Cabinet Government's Beauty . . . Lies in Being No More Than Skin Deep," *National Journal*, vol. 17 (June 15, 1985).

Kirschten, Dick. "Reagan Gets Unsolicited Advice on His Personnel Appointments," *National Journal*, vol. 17 (December 14, 1985).

Kirschten, Dick. "Reagan's Cabinet Councils May Have Less Influence Than Meets the Eye," *National Journal*, vol. 13 (July 11, 1981).

Lanouette, William J. "SES—From Civil Service Showpiece to Incipient Failure in Two Years," *National Journal*, vol. 13 (July 18, 1981).

Lemman, Nicholas. "How Carter Fails: Taking the Politics Out of Government," *The Washington Monthly* (September 1978).

Light, Larry. "Carter's Year," *Congressional Quarterly* (January 5, 1980).

Lowi, Theodore J. "Four Systems of Policy, Politics and Choice," *Public Administration Review*, vol. 32 (1972).

Lynn, Laurence E., Jr. "Manager's Role in Public Management," *The Bureaucrat*, vol. 13 (Winter 1984).

Lynn, Naomi B., and Evaden, Richard. "Bureaucratic Responses to Civil Service Reform," *Public Administration Review*, vol. 38 (July/August 1979).

MacKenzie, G. Calvin. "Cabinet and Subcabinet Personnel Selections in Reagan's First Year: New Variations on Some Not-So-Old Themes," paper presented at the Annual Meeting of the American Political Science Association, New York City (September 2–5, 1982).

MacKenzie, G. Calvin. "Personnel Selection for a Conservative Administration: The Reagan Experience 1980–81," unpublished paper.

Mansfield, Harvey C. "Federal Executive Reorganization: Thirty Years Experience," *Public Administration Review*, vol. 29 (1969).

Mansfield, Harvey C. "Reorganizing the Federal Executive Branch: The Limits of Institutionalization," *Law and Contemporary Problems*, vol. 35 (1970).

McCaffery, Jerry. "MBO and the Federal Budgeting Process," *Public Administration Review*, vol. 36 (1976).

McCurdy, Howard E. *Public Administration: A Synthesis* (Menlo Park, N.J.: Cummings, 1977).

Miroff, Bruce. *Pragmatic Illusions* (New York: David McKay, 1976).

Moyers, Bill. "Carter Interview," *Congressional Quarterly Weekly Report* (November 25, 1978).

Mullen, William F. *Presidential Power and Politics* (New York: St. Martin's Press, 1976).

Nachmias, David, and Nachmias, Chiva. *Research Methods in the Social Sciences* (New York: St. Martin's Press, 1976).

Nathan, Richard P. *The Plot That Failed* (New York: John Wiley, 1975).

Neustadt, Richard. "Approaches to Staffing the Presidency: Notes on FDR and JFK," *American Political Science Review*, vol. 57 (1963).

Neustadt, Richard. *Presidential Power* (New York: John Wiley, 1960).

Newland, Chester A. "The Reagan Presidency: Limited Government and Political Administration," *Public Administration Review*, vol. 43 (January/February 1983).

News Conference Text (May 8, 1978). *Congressional Quarterly Weekly Report* (July 20, 1978).

News Conference Text (July 20, 1978). *Congressional Quarterly Weekly Report* (July 29, 1978).

Osborne, John. "Fluff: Staff Changes," *The New Republic* (May 7, 1978).

Ostrum, Vincent. *The Intellectual Crisis in American Public Administration* (University, Ala.: University of Alabama Press, 1973).

Palmer, John L., and Mills, Gregory B. "Budget Policy," in *The Reagan Experiment*, John L. Palmer and Isabel V. Sawhill, eds. (Washington, D.C.: Urban Institute Press, 1982).

Palmer, John L., and Sawhill, Isabel V., eds. *The Reagan Experiment* (Washington, D.C.: Urban Institute Press, 1982).

Pfiffer, James P. "Budgeting and the 'People's Reform,' " *Public Administration Review*, vol. 40 (March/April 1980).

Pious, Richard M. *The American Presidency* (New York: Basic Books, 1979).

Polenberg, Richard. *Reorganizing Roosevelt's Government* (Cambridge: Harvard University Press, 1966).

Presidential News Conference. *Congressional Quarterly Weekly Report* (May 6, 1978).

Reed, Leonard. "The Bureaucracy: The Cleverest Lobby of Them All," *The Washington Monthly* (April 1978).

Ripley, Randall B., and Franklin, Grace A. *Congress, the Bureaucracy, and Public Policy* (Homewood, Ill.: Dorsey Press, 1976).

Rose, Richard. *Managing Presidential Objectives* (New York: Free Press, 1976).

Rosen, Bernard. "A Disaster for Merit," *The Bureaucrat*, vol. 11 (Winter 1982–83).

Rossiter, Clinton. *The American Presidency*, rev. ed. (New York: New American Library, 1960).

Salomon, Jean-Jacques. *Science and Politics* (Cambridge: MIT Press, 1973).

Sayre, Wallace S. "Premises of Public Administration," *Public Administration Review*, vol. 8 (1948).

Schick, Allen. "The Battle of the Budget," in *Congress Against the Presidency*, Harvey C. Mansfield, ed. (New York: Praeger, 1975).

Schick, Allen. "A Death in the Bureaucracy: The Demise of Federal PPB," *Public Administration Review*, vol. 29 (1969).

Schick, Allen. "The Road From ZBB," *Public Administration Review*, vol. 38 (March/April 1978).

Schick, Allen. "Systems, Politics, and Systems Budgeting," *Public Administration Review*, vol. 29 (1969).

Schick, Allen. "The Trauma of Politics: Public Administration in the Sixties," in *American Public Administration: Past, Present, Future*, Frederick Mosher, ed. (University, Ala.: University of Alabama Press, 1974).

Schlesinger, Arthur M., Jr. *The Imperial Presidency* (New York: Houghton Mifflin, 1973).

Schlesinger, Arthur M., Jr. *A Thousand Days* (New York: Fawcett, 1965).

Simon, Herbert. *Administrative Behavior* (New York: Macmillan, 1957).

Sin, R. G. H. "The Craft of Power," quoted in "Subverting the Subterraneans," *National Journal*, vol. 8 (1976).

Stanfield, Rochelle. "At Least It Didn't Cost Much," *National Journal*, vol. 11 (June 2, 1979).

Stanfield, Rochelle. "The Best Laid Reorganization Plans Sometimes Go Astray," *National Journal*, vol. 11 (January 20, 1979).

Stanfield, Rochelle. "The Reorganization Staff Is Big Loser in the Latest Shuffle," *National Journal*, vol. 11 (March 10, 1979).

Stockman, David. *The Triumph of Politics: Why the Reagan Revolution Failed* (New York: Harper and Row, 1986).

Sundquist, James L. "Jimmy Carter as Public Administrator: An Appraisal at Midterm," *Public Administration Review*, vol. 39 (January/February 1979).

Tolley, Howard. *Children and War: Socialization to International Conflict* (New York: Teachers College Press, 1973).

Thayer, Frederick. "The President's Management Reforms: Theory X Triumphant," *Public Administration Review*, vol. 38 (July/August 1978).

U.S. Department of Commerce. *Historical Statistics of the United States* (Washington, D.C.: Department of Commerce, 1976).

Waldo, Dwight. *The Administrative State* (New York: Ronald Press, 1948).

Waldo, Dwight. "Public Administration," *International Encyclopedia of the Social Sciences*, vol. 13 (New York: Macmillan and Free Press, 1948).

Wann, A. J. *The President as Chief Administrator: A Study of Franklin D. Roosevelt* (Washington, D.C.: Public Affairs Press, 1968).

White House Report. "Jordan's New Role Signals an End to 'Cabinet Government,'" *National Journal*, vol. 11 (August 18, 1979).

White House Report. "The Power Vacuum Outside the Oval Office," *National Journal*, vol. 10 (February 24, 1978).

White, Leonard. *Introduction to the Study of Administration* (New York: Macmillan, 1929).

Wildavsky, Aaron. *The Politics of the Budgetary Process* (Boston: Little, Brown, 1974).

Wines, Michael. "Administration, Critics Play Legal Cat and Mouse on Agency Rules," *National Journal*, vol. 14 (December 18, 1982).

Wines, Michael. "Reagan's Reforms Are Full of Sound and Fury, but What Do They Signify?" *National Journal*, vol. 14 (January 16, 1982).

Wolfenstein, Victor E. "The Two Wars of Lyndon Johnson," *Politics and Society*, vol. 3 (December 1974).

Woll, Peter, and Jones, Rochelle. "Against One-Man Rule: Bureaucratic Defense in Depth," *The Nation*, vol. 217 (1973).

Notes on Methodology

Data for the empirical investigation of the Carter and Reagan management programs presented in Chapters 6 and 7 were gathered through two sets of mail questionnaires sent to administrative officials in the federal bureaucracy during the Carter and Reagan administrations. The sample of administrative executives was drawn from *The Federal Executive Telephone Directory* obtained from the Office of Personnel Management. The directory lists the names and job titles of all executives for the major cabinet departments and administrative agencies. Executives were chosen on the basis of their job title. Executives in administrative capacities were chosen for the sample because it was felt they would best be able to evaluate the effectiveness of Carter and Reagan management techniques and leadership skills. The executives for the Reagan survey were, whenever possible, chosen from the same positions used in the Carter survey. However, because of reductions in force and vacancies in positions, that was not always possible; therefore, the Reagan sample is slightly smaller than the Carter sample.

The survey of executives during the Carter administration was administered in the summer of 1980. Four hundred fifty questionnaires were mailed and 212 executives (47 percent) filled out and returned the questionnaire. The Reagan survey was administered in the summer of 1984, with 430 questionnaires mailed to administrative executives and 150 (35 percent) returned. In both surveys, responses were received from all domestic departments and all administrative agencies. While the larger departments and administrative agencies obviously dominated the return, the response sample was representative of the survey sample. However, the response samples for both surveys were dominated by career civil servants. Ninety-five percent of the 1980 respondents and 90 percent of the 1984 respondents were career civil servants. A greater mix of political executives and career civil servants was hoped for so that the returns could be broken down by career status. However, because career executives so clearly dominated the universe, this was impossible. "Eyeballing" the data suggests that, as expected, the political appointees evaluated the presidents' programs and leadership skills more positively in both administrations. However, the cell sizes are so small that comparisons are probably not very valid, and therefore the data are not presented here.

Both surveys were administered during an election year, primarily because of convenience more than design. It was feared that the sensitive nature of the questions, combined with the timing, might inhibit the respondents. Obviously, the response rates and the evaluations indicate that this was not the case. Instead, the questions seemed to strike a responsive chord among those surveyed.

The decision to rely on mail questionnaires rather than interviews for gathering data was originally made with some trepidation. The primary problem with mail questionnaires is a low response rate, resulting in an inability to generalize. However, a variety of techniques, such as follow-up mailings, personalized cover letters, self-addressed stamped return envelopes, postcard reminders/thank you notes, and respondent anonymity, can be used to increase response rates. All these techniques were used in both surveys. Given the response rates, the techniques must have been successful since acceptable response rates for mail surveys generally run from 20 to 40 percent. However, even using these techniques, the response rate for the Reagan survey lagged behind the response rate for the Carter survey. Handwritten notes accompanying the questionnaires suggested that federal executives have been inundated with questionnaires and are therefore increasingly less likely to respond to them.

A second disadvantage of mail questionnaires concerns the validity of the respondent; that is, how can the researcher be certain the questionnaire is filled out by the person to whom it is sent. Originally it was felt that this might be a problem. However, there were so many personalized responses accompanying the returns (including margin notes, handwritten notes on separate paper, and so on) that the validity of the respondents was easily settled.

However, even given the problems associated with mail questionnaires, when used correctly, they are a wonderful research tool that enables the researcher to gather a breadth of data impossible to gather in any other way. In research areas such as the presidency, where empirical data has been extremely difficult to obtain, mail questionnaires provide a unique opportunity.

Index

About the Author

JAMES G. BENZE, JR., is Assistant Professor of Political Science, Washington and Jefferson College. He has published articles on national and state campaigns and elections as well as presidential management in such scholarly journals as *Presidential Studies Quarterly, Social Science Quarterly,* and *Journalism Quarterly.*